WHERE THERE'S A HILL

ONE WOMAN, 214 LAKE DISTRICT FELLS,

WHERE

FOUR ATTEMPTS, ONE RECORD-BREAKING

THERE'S

WAINWRIGHTS RUN

A HILL

SABRINA VERJEE

Vertebrate Publishing, Sheffield
www.adventurebooks.com

WHERE THERE'S A HILL

SABRINA VERJEE

First published in 2022 by Vertebrate Publishing.

 Vertebrate Publishing, Omega Court, 352 Cemetery Road,
Sheffield S11 8FT, United Kingdom.
www.adventurebooks.com

Front cover photo: James Appleton.
Map illustrations: Simon Norris.
Other photography as credited.

This book is a work of non-fiction based on the life of Sabrina Verjee. The author has stated to the publishers that, except in such minor respects not affecting the substantial accuracy of the work, the contents of the book are true.

A CIP catalogue record for this book is available from the British Library.

ISBN: 978-1-83981-146-3 (Paperback)
ISBN: 978-1-83981-147-0 (Ebook)
ISBN: 978-1-83981-148-7 (Audiobook)

10 9 8 7 6 5 4 3 2 1

Mapping contains data from OS © Crown copyright and database right (2021) and © OpenStreetMap contributors, *Openstreetmap.org/copyright*
Relief shading produced from data derived from U.S. Geological Survey, National Geospatial Program.
Cartography by Richard Ross, Active Maps Ltd.

Edited by Ed Douglas.
Cover design by Jane Beagley, layout and production by Rosie Edwards, Vertebrate Publishing.
www.adventurebooks.com

Vertebrate Publishing is committed to printing on paper from sustainable sources.

Printed and bound in Great Britain by Clays Ltd., Elcograf S.p.A.

To my support team – you're the best!

From the bottom of my heart, thank you to each and every
one of you that gave up your time to help me. From the first
attempt to the record-breaking round, you all had a part to play.
I have wonderful memories of the times we shared together in
the hills and support points and I will cherish these forever.

CONTENTS

ONE DON'T COME LAST 1

TWO TAKE A DEEP BREATH 15

THREE GOING THE DISTANCE 25

FOUR THE WRECKED AND THE DAMNED 41

FIVE BREAKING THE LAW? 51

SIX READY, STEADY, STOP! 61

SEVEN LEAN ON ME 77

EIGHT BROKEN 95

NINE THIRD TIME LUCKY? 109

TEN BREATHE EASY 123

ELEVEN FOURTH TIME LUCKY 141

EPILOGUE 155

ACKNOWLEDGEMENTS 163

ABOUT THE AUTHOR 167

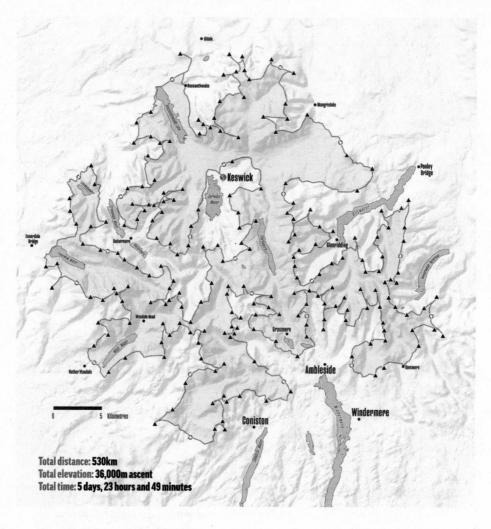

Total distance: 530km
Total elevation: 36,000m ascent
Total time: 5 days, 23 hours and 49 minutes

The route Sabrina took in 2021 when she set a new record for visiting all 214 Wainwright summits in one continuous journey on foot.

ONE
DON'T COME LAST

I was not a natural athlete. In my early school years I was terrible at sports. All of them. I went to a primary school called Danesfield where, twice a week, we went outside for sports lessons, usually on the hard-surface playground. Most commonly we played netball, but in the summer months there were games of rounders too. I had barely touched a ball in my life until I went to school. My parents had no interest in sport whatsoever and my first and only opportunity to play any was in these twice-weekly school sessions.

It seems unthinkable now but the teachers thought it appropriate to select two children who would then get to pick their own team, and there were usually three of us left over at the end who didn't get chosen at all. We had to sit on the bench and watch the other kids play. The difference was that while I was desperate to join in, the other two hated sports. Even worse, the teachers went down the list in alphabetical order, so I never even had the chance to be the captain, given how low in the alphabet the name Sabrina is. Silly parents. Why couldn't they have called me something more useful, like Anna?

This is one example from many of how my early schooldays were a bit miserable. Just as I was left out of official sports, I was also left out of the informal playground games the other children occupied themselves with at lunch break. I never understood why I was excluded. I was a quiet child but also confident. I would go up to a group of children playing and ask if I could join in, but they would say no and never seemed to have an explanation as to why not. So I amused myself. I would go to the edge of the playground where there was soil and trees, and I would look at the insects and play with the twigs and spiders on my own. In the end, I decided that lunch break and playtime were quite boring, so one day I went back into the classroom to sit at a desk and do my homework. When a teacher discovered me doing this, I got a severe telling off.

'Homework is to be done at home!' she yelled at me. 'Go back out to the playground and play!'

I knew I was different from the other children, but never really understood why. As an adult I do look back and wonder if it had anything to do with the colour of my skin. I remember when another 'brown' child came to our school and it seemed to be a big thing. Especially when he decided to do a poo on the school lawn. I suppose I thought people treated him differently because of that behaviour rather than his colour. I felt sorry for him. He was treated like an outcast. I would have made friends with him but he was two years below me. Other than us two, my school was all white. There were eighteen girls in my year and only three boys. And one of them wanted to be a girl. I liked him. He was kind and quite funny but didn't like playing sport, so I was always annoyed when they picked him to play on the netball team instead of me. He didn't want to play and I did.

It can't have been easy for my parents being immigrants in the UK in the 1970s and 1980s, but they presented themselves simply as two hard-working people who minded their own business. My mum, Christine, is French. She was in the UK from a young age but I've always found it hard to extract the facts about her childhood. I know she went to a French lycée in London to study. I also know she had to leave school early to look after my grandmother, who was mentally unwell. She lived in a flat in central London, where my grandfather was the boss for Lancôme.

My mum has blonde hair and blue eyes, so I would I say I look more like my dad. Mum met my dad, Azad, when she was sixteen and they were both working at a grocery store. He was ten years older.

Dad was born in Nairobi in Kenya. His great-great-grandfather, together with his great-great-grandfather's five brothers, left India in 1886, travelling from Bombay in a dhow. They arrived in Mombasa and established a business there connected to the migrant labour building the railway. Dad came to Britain to study for his A-levels but dropped out and instead became a chef in a restaurant. I think my French grandfather must have been a bit racist. He disowned my mum when she wanted to marry 'an Indian'. I suspect, though, there was more to it than that. I think Mum was his favourite daughter and he didn't want to let her leave. She had two younger sisters who she looked after as well. And despite initially turning his back on her, when my sister was born, my grandfather eventually accepted my mum's decision to marry my father and they had a good relationship after that. My mum was indeed still the favourite.

Dad speaks Gujarati fluently but has still never been to India. I got him to teach me a bit of Gujarati when I was little and I think I could count and say a few words, but I've forgotten it all now. He was very upset when, having read our children's version of the Bible, I told him that I didn't think God existed. He would say he is an Ismaili except he drinks alcohol, eats pork and never goes to mosque. My dad is sweet and empathetic, the most huggable person I know. He's also the tallest in the family, at five foot six, with my sister and me vying for shortest at around five foot two.

My sister, Natasha, is a couple of years older than me. By the time she was born, my parents were living in a flat in the corner shop they'd opened in the Surrey village of Hersham, close to Walton-on-Thames. This would have been in the late 1970s. By the time I was born, two years later, they had moved to their own house in Cobham, where they still live. When my sister was a baby, my mum spoke to her in French, but then my dad complained that when my sister started talking he couldn't understand her, so he banned French from the house. I always think it is so sad I didn't get to learn French when I was little; it would have been so easy for me at school. Instead, I had to learn it the hard way, like all the other children. That's the main reason I rarely tell people that I am half French, because naturally they expect me to speak the language like a mother tongue and I can't. My sister, who now lives in Denmark, is extremely gifted in picking up languages – not just French but also Danish, German and Italian.

My sister was definitely better at sport than me when we were young. She actually had some ball skills. She played netball and is pretty good at tennis. She would get bored of playing tennis with me because I was so bad, and would wander off, even though I was enjoying myself. When we were younger and had family over for barbecues or Christmas, I was always the shy, introverted one. I'd disappear off into the woods for a little adventure on my own to escape the 'family'. I found it really intimidating to have these relatives round that I didn't know that well. I never had anything to say to them. Natasha was such a chatterbox that she loved it. She was generally a very amiable person and had lots of friends at school.

I've been called a 'Paki' a few times in my life. As a kid, that really confused me, because not only did I not know what a Paki was but when I asked my parents to explain they told me that I was not Pakistani but half Indian and half French. I thought my dad was Kenyan. When a teacher at school had asked me where I was from, I told her 'Surrey'. When she probed a bit more and asked about my dad, I told her he was from Kenya. Then she became confused as to why I was brown and not black.

Many years later, when I was working as a locum vet in Luton, a white couple came in with their cat. They were drunk and having a domestic. In fact, they got so angry they were scaring their cat, so I asked them to wait outside. I treated their cat and gave it back to them and thought no more about it. But some weeks later, the company I was working for asked me to respond to a complaint. It basically accused me of being a Pakistani and of stealing a British person's job. There was nothing there about the work I had done or my communication with them. It was simply that they hadn't paid the bill and wanted an excuse not to. I didn't know whether to be more shocked by the racists who wrote the letter or the person who had asked me to respond to it.

As a person, I embrace everyone, no matter where they are from, what their sexual orientation is, what religious beliefs they have or what they do for a living. I completely ignore hierarchy and status. To me, all people are equal. I then judge them on how they behave, although I am getting better about being more forgiving when people behave in ways that I don't agree with. I think I am this way because of my multicultural background and because I don't feel I have a skin colour I identify with: I'm just a person. I do wish that I had more of a cultural identity so I had a sense of belonging to a 'group'.

I was lucky that I had a stable family life. My parents worked hard but I think they were happy. My sister and I would often sit in the car outside the shop, waiting for them to finish work. They served a community of people and so I think they were accepted, but I wonder what impact being disowned by her father had on my mother. It tells you something about her resilient nature: her stubbornness, thick skin and ability to thrive even when everything around her is trying to drag her down. I still call my parents' home 'home'. I am very lucky to feel so at ease when I'm with my parents, despite us being worlds apart in what we enjoy doing. They are the most amazing comfort blanket. I do think that my confidence, self-belief, independence and ability to risk failure are down to them. They never put pressure on me to be anything; they only ever want me to be happy and have no expectations.

Sometimes, though, I wonder if my motivation to achieve comes from a desire to make them proud or attract their attention. I remember when I was a child I would hear other parents bragging about their children, how talented they were, and I'd be thinking that was weird because I was better than their child at that particular thing but my mum never said those things about me. I would come home with various trophies, for things like being the best at maths in my class, and the trophy would just be kept in my bag and barely acknowledged. There was definitely more focus on the things I wasn't so good at, like swimming. The number of times as an adult I have had to sit and relive the experience as my mum and sister giggle describing the fiasco of getting me into the pool. I had to put a nose-clip on, earplugs, armbands and a rubber ring, and even then I was terrified. It's quite funny now that I'm actually quite a strong swimmer, having learnt quickly when I started modern pentathlon at Oxford.

I think I would have hated school if it weren't for my academic abilities. As it turned out, I was actually very good at maths and English, and best in my class at most things. Unfortunately, having done all the work I'd been given, I'd then get bored while all the other children were still working at it. I would then start being 'naughty' and get in trouble. My entire school career was a mixture of praise for my academic achievements alternating with being scolded for my naughtiness. The teachers didn't know what to do with me, so decided to put me up a year to be with children a year older than me. They also did this to split me up from my first and newly made friend, who was, apparently, being corrupted by my misbehaviour. So in this new academic year I had no friends. On top of that, I was getting relatively worse in the sports department since I was now competing against children a year older than me. I had been the shortest child in the class I'd just left, so you can imagine the difference. My parents would come to sports day begging me to not come last in just one race. My best effort was third from last in the egg and spoon race. At least that got them off my case.

The following year, my new class reached the end of primary school. I should have gone with them to secondary school but I was only ten and none of the secondary schools wanted me. I was too young. Great! What to do now? The teachers decided it would be best for me to repeat the final academic year. So now I was back with the children in my previous year group, except now they hated me even more for being a clever clogs. There was no point even trying to make friends any more.

Secondary school wasn't much better. Once again I found myself in and out of the headmistress's office, alternating between being congratulated for winning a prize in a poetry competition and being told off for writing a rude poem about a teacher during class. I wasn't happy. I found it hard to make friends and although I enjoyed my academic work, I also wanted to be outside doing sports. I learnt to play tennis but was quickly excluded from the school's elitist club because I simply wasn't good enough. 'Only the best girls will be able to play tennis,' I was told.

I thought of the twin sisters in my year who ran the 400 metres. Running sounded like fun. Maybe I could do that. There was a grass athletics track on the school playing fields with white lanes painted round the oval 200-metre circuit. Once a week in summer we had a 'track session', which was timed for a 100-metre or 200-metre run. I remember being very slow to get off the start. In the first second, I seemed to be five metres behind the others and my chest would close up on me. I literally couldn't breathe. As the first girl crossed the line, I was still only halfway. What was wrong with me? The 200-metre races were slightly less embarrassing. I would still have a slow start, but right at the end I would be starting to close the gap. True, I'd still finish last, but I could at least produce a result that was worth recording. I thought to myself that if the race were longer, I would have more time to catch up.

I loved being outside. At some point my mum decided she preferred to work on her own, and so it was more often Dad who did the daily parenting. Playing with dollies was forbidden and if caught we'd be sent outside to play in the woods, where we would make shelters out of branches and bracken and play imaginary games, like pretending we owned our own riding stables. We would role-play booking clients for lessons and then pretend that they were arriving and that we'd help them choose a horse and teach them to ride.

This fantasy stemmed from our experiences at the local riding stables. With our parents so busy at work, it was handy for them to drop us at the stables, where we would work mucking horses out, bringing them in from the fields, turning them out to grass, grooming them, tacking them up for wealthy clients, polishing the leather tack afterwards and sweeping the yard. My sister and I would graft all day long during the holidays and weekends, from 8 a.m. to 8 p.m. We were the most diligent, hard-working kids. And we loved it. We were rewarded for our labours with 'free rides' on the ponies. We had our favourites, and mine were always the fast and frisky ones. I would often fall off, since the badly behaved horses would rear and buck. The reward of a more dangerous ride was the thrill of speed. Natasha preferred the safer rides and it annoyed me when we went on a hack if I had to wait for her slower horse. Then again, she would laugh at me when I fell off, although as the older sister she always took care of me. Sometimes we'd have to catch and retrieve my pony, which wasn't always easy. If it took a while, we would arrive back late to the yard, sometimes at dusk and without lights. We had such fun at the stables and for my parents it was free babysitting.

The yard owner would put pressure on us to get there as early as possible so we could get the horses ready for lessons. We were happy to oblige but my dad never liked getting out of bed early. We would ask him the night before if we could please leave at 7.30 a.m. and he would say, 'Okay, but you have to bring me a cup of tea to my bedroom to wake me up and then you need to do the household chores.' The list of chores grew longer and longer. It started with emptying the dishwasher, but the next week we were also raking the leaves off the lawn and sweeping the drive, then on top of that we were combing the tassels on the sitting-room rug, a job I hated since it seemed so pointless. We knew Dad was just trying to keep us busy in the morning so he could have a lie-in.

Looking back now, I realise my poor father was just exhausted. He's not always had the best of health, but as children we couldn't understand why he wouldn't get out of bed when all he had to do was drive us to the stables. We were getting up earlier and earlier to get the ever-growing list of chores done just so we could go to the stables to provide more slave labour. It's quite funny in retrospect. Health and safety these days would never allow children to do the things we did. We had so much freedom and independence. Once we discovered how to cycle properly and were bought two good mountain bikes, my sister and I could ride to the stables ourselves and no longer had to rely on our dad. I think we would have been around twelve and fourteen years old at that point. I loved cycling. It made me self-reliant. Until then, because our house was a few miles from Cobham village centre, we hadn't been able to reach any shops on our own.

When it came to choosing my A-levels, I was very disappointed to be told I couldn't do chemistry or biology as I'd only done the dual award science for my GCSE option. I discussed the situation with my parents and suggested I might be better off going to a different school. And could I please go to boarding school? I investigated the different options and decided I liked the look of Charterhouse in Godalming, a very prestigious school. In those days, Charterhouse was more or less boys only, but they allowed up to twenty-one girls in for A-levels to pull up the school's grades. I convinced my parents it was a great idea. They wouldn't have to chauffeur me to and from school or the train station, which I knew annoyed them.

They agreed that if I passed the admission test they would give me their blessing.

Charterhouse changed my life. Instead of being excluded, I was automatically included in groups. As girls we were divided into two boarding houses, or 'digs', where we slept in our first year. During the day we were part of the boys' boarding houses: three girls in each A-level year group. Mine was called Hodgsonites. In the morning we attended chapel where we sang hymns. I loved singing. I would learn the words and sing as loud and as well as I could. The choirmaster approached me one morning and said he could hear my voice and that I was talented and should have lessons. Being a cynical teenager, I thought he just wanted some more work: my parents would have to pay for these lessons. But I wanted to try and see if it was fun. I was too nervous to make a sound and suggested I might be more comfortable whistling. So we started with that. Gradually I found my voice and eventually went on to sing in some solo competitions on stage in front of lots of people. Despite my fear, it was good to push myself and my confidence grew.

I was also actively encouraged to do every single sport imaginable. I learnt how to rock climb on the school's indoor climbing wall. There were house teams for hockey, basketball, mixed lacrosse and football, and whenever an extra team member was required, I would step in. I knew I wasn't very good, but no one seemed to mind. Playing football, I discovered that while I still didn't have any ball skills, I could be quite useful at defence. I would sprint from one end of the pitch to the other, trying to intercept the ball, and could just keep going for the full ninety minutes. Towards the end of the game, when everyone was fatigued, I began to get to the ball first because everyone else simply gave up. It was my moment to shine. Except, having finally got the ball, I'd try to kick it several times without really sending it anywhere. But at least that amused everybody else and it didn't matter to me because at last I was able to join in and have fun.

Every year Charterhouse held a six-kilometre cross-country race round the grounds and every pupil had to compete. I was really excited about it, but half of the students weren't keen at all and thought it far too long.

My friends Lindsey and Rebecca were a bit nervous about the distance and suggested we all run together for moral support. At the beginning of the race they had to slow down to wait for me as I struggled to keep up, but from about halfway it was definitely the other way round. I had not run that far before, but it felt easy. When we reached the dreaded Jacob's ladder (a large number of steps through the wood), I was shocked to find how easily I bounded up them, given that I was always the slowest when we went up them on the way back from town at the weekends.

Best of all, I was allowed to study whatever I wanted and was praised for my academic ability. I chose biology, chemistry, maths and economics and excelled at all of them. I was thrilled to be selected by the school as a candidate for Oxbridge, but because I was having so much fun at Charterhouse those two years went all too quickly and I didn't manage to fill in a UCAS form or make any decisions about my future. Before I knew it, the end of school was nigh and while all my friends had places at universities, I was embarking on an unplanned gap year.

Determined not to waste a year, I decided to join a Raleigh International expedition to Ghana. It was a bit of a battle persuading my parents. Perhaps understandably, they didn't want their daughter going to Africa without them for three months. I explained I would be raising money for charity and building a school. The next hurdle was raising the £2,000 to sign up. I tried everything. I ordered biros with 'I sponsored Raleigh International' etched into them, except half the biros didn't work and I was too embarrassed to sell them. At a cousin's suggestion, I wrote to twenty-five local companies looking for sponsorship, and to my uncle's company in London too. One of the local companies sent me £25 and my uncle sent me £500.

With my own savings I was halfway there. My grandfather had bought some shares for me when I was young and I had kept an eye on the price of them over the years. They seemed to go up and down on a daily basis. It occurred to me that if I bought shares at the right time when the price was low and sold them at a peak, I could make a lot of money. The problem was that I wasn't yet eighteen and couldn't legally trade shares. So I asked my parents. They explained there were brokerage fees involved and I would have to consider this when buying and selling. For a few weeks I checked the FTSE 100 in the newspaper and then, hedging my bets, bought shares in the National Grid, an oil company (I can't remember which one now) and Santander. I watched their prices avidly and after three months sold them for a profit of £300. Most of that came from Santander.

The rest of the money I made up working at my mum's grocery shop, Cullens, in central London, which she'd run since my parents had sold the corner shop so Dad could open his own restaurant. (My mum had ended up buying Cullens and ran it on her own.) I also made some cash escorting hacks at the local riding school. With only one month to go, I signed up for the trip and got all the relevant travel information, including the vaccinations I needed. I had to ask my parents to pay for the jabs and it dawned on them that I was committed to going, which they still weren't happy about. But before they could change their minds, they were dropping me at Heathrow. It was different in those days: no mobile phones. The only way they could communicate with me was on the group's satellite phone. We were allowed only one phone call each for the three-month trip and that was going to have to be on A-level results day.

I learnt a lot about myself in Ghana. There were twenty-seven of us, split into three groups of nine. We spent a week in Accra all together and then we went off to three different projects. My group was assigned to build a school first. I absolutely loved the physical labour, something I had only seen adult men do before. I would wake up and be first out on the foundations. We had to remove rocks from the ground and dig out trenches. I would grab the wheelbarrow and start digging, but when it was full I couldn't lift it on my own and I'd have to ask someone to help me. I found my muscles swelling and became rather proud of my biceps.

While grafting, I hadn't paid much attention to what the others got up to. We got together for breaks and mealtimes, taking it in turns to cook and wash up. There was some grumbling about one or two in the group who didn't seem to pull their weight, but it didn't particularly bother me. Everything always got done and I was happy doing what was needed. At the end of the project, we all sat in a circle and our group leader said we should think of something to say about each of our fellow team members. It was a bit daunting, waiting to be told what people thought of you. And I was surprised people thought I was intimidating. I'm really small, quite quiet and generally keep myself to myself. So I couldn't understand why people were scared of me. They also said I had this inner self-motivation to get jobs done and this had inspired them to do the same. I couldn't understand why they weren't all self-motivated too. We were there to build a school and I wanted to build it as quickly as possible. I enjoyed seeing the fruits of our labour and was immensely proud of our teamwork.

Coming home from Ghana, I realised I had caught the travel bug, so I took as many jobs as I could to raise funds. I worked weekdays for a temping agency, answering phones, typing and even working on presentations. The work was varied and I found it exciting to try out different jobs. In the evenings I waitressed at various pubs and restaurants. Sometimes I would finish at 3 a.m. but I would still manage to get up for the day job. On the weekends I worked at a riding school, mucking out stables or leading children out for a hack. Then in the evenings I would head straight to the restaurant for my waitressing job. I must have been working an average of 100 hours a week and didn't get much sleep. My parents were amazing. My mum always made sure there was a meal ready or something I could stick in the microwave. I really have no idea what they thought about my lifestyle choices, but I think they were proud of how hard I was working. In the middle of all this, I managed to fill in the UCAS forms and got a place at St Anne's College, Oxford to study human sciences.

In January 2000 I headed off to Peru for more charitable work abroad. I was sent to a Lunahuaná, a small town by the Cañete river, where I taught English to willing students with another English girl. After our placement was over, we travelled together for a month, riding donkeys out of Colca Canyon, the world's second-deepest gorge, and walking the Inca Trail. We didn't bother with guides, just made our way to the start of the trail and kept going all the way to Machu Picchu. It was an incredible experience; we hadn't trained but were so used to carrying heavy backpacks that it all felt quite normal apart from some mild altitude sickness, but a local gave us some coca leaves to chew on and this helped a lot.

After returning home from South America, I went straight back to my 100-hour week to earn more money for more adventure travelling. That summer I went to St Petersburg with my friend Charlotte and we took the Trans-Siberian train all the way to Irkutsk and camped round the shores of Lake Baikal. After that we headed south to Ulaanbaatar, the capital of Mongolia. We hiked and rode horses, camping most nights. When Charlotte went home, another friend came out to join me and we continued exploring, hiking across the country with maps and backpacks, making our way to Kazakhstan and Kyrgyzstan before returning to the UK.

I spent the next three years at Oxford, studying hard but also trying lots of sports. I joined the Oxford University Women's Lightweight Rowing Club squad and after an intense eight-week training camp was as fit and lean as I have ever been. We had eleven training sessions a week and one of them was an hour of running. This was the first time I'd run properly. By the end of the camp I was the second-fastest runner on the squad. I enjoyed rowing and the hard training programme, but I didn't enjoy the politics. It was made clear that I wouldn't get a place for the boat race, despite being the most reliable and attentive member of the team. My power-to-weight ratio was good and I knew I could improve my technique, but it soon became clear from the other girls that I didn't belong there.

Luckily for me, I had somewhere else to go: Oxford's modern pentathlon team. I hadn't even heard of the pentathlon until a friend asked me to join the St Anne's team so we could compete. At the time I could ride a horse and run three kilometres, but I wasn't a good swimmer, had only shot a rifle and not a pistol, and had definitely never held a sword before. I threw myself at the sport with all my passion, motivation and rigour, learning to swim with a more efficient stroke and working on my speed. I learnt how to fence épée and became a pretty reliable pistol shooter. Unlike rowing, I enjoyed the social side of pentathlon as well. And I was proud to earn my status as a half-blue in representing Oxford.

Throughout my childhood, I had always been good with numbers and every career questionnaire had me as an accountant or banker. So, despite studying science, it was no surprise the banks found me. A small group of us would regularly be wined and dined by various banks – Goldman Sachs, Deutsche, UBS – on the 'milk round' to recruit bright graduates. In the summer of my second year, I had an internship in the mergers and acquisitions department of Credit Suisse First Boston in London's Canary Wharf. They offered me a job, to start when I graduated, but I quickly realised I was in the wrong place. Although I enjoyed the work, I couldn't sit in a chair for longer than ten minutes. I didn't enjoy the office politics either and one day, sitting at my desk, I wondered what it was I really wanted to do: something outdoors where I could use my brain. I decided there and then I wanted be an equine vet. And so I resigned.

My mum couldn't hide her disappointment. She thought the banking job was a great career, something she would have liked to aspire to. She's a very astute business lady with a head for figures, but without A-levels her education was cut short. But I had made up my mind. And I never looked back.

TWO

TAKE A DEEP BREATH

I remember the CEO from Credit Suisse First Boston calling me on my mobile the day after I quit my job. He could not believe anyone would do such a thing. How could anyone go from being a top earner on a great career path to being a student again? He tried to get me back but I had made my decision. And in any case I'd already travelled up to the Lake District for a fun mountain adventure, hiking and camping. When I came back refreshed, I got straight on to finding another job to tide me over until vet school started in nine months. I moved out of my grandparents' flat in London, where I'd been living while working at the bank, and into the top floor of a farmhouse in Surrey, swapping a well-paid City job for poorly paid work in a stables. I was instantly happier.

My room was part of my wages plus £100 per week and permission to keep my childhood pony Magic in one of the fields. My room's skylights had no blinds and I loved waking up in the morning with the beams of sunlight shining through. There is something about the colour green and the fresh smells of the outdoors, the tangibility of the weather, being a part of nature. It was incredibly relaxing and refreshing, and in stark contrast to the grey, concrete, hard world of cities and banks. I could see out to acres of fields sprinkled with horses. It was a simple life: taking off their indoor rugs and putting on the outdoor ones before turning them out to their fields. We would then muck out all the stables before lunch. In the afternoon we would exercise the horses on treks through the fields and on the local network of bridleways, which I particularly enjoyed. Then we would groom them all before putting them back to bed.

During this time, I applied to various vet schools and accepted an offer to study at St Edmund's College, Cambridge. I had five more amazing university years to indulge my passion for sport. I competed for Cambridge in the modern pentathlon, triathlon, cycling and cross-country running. I was also introduced to adventure racing, although not through the university. I joined CamRacers, the local adventure-racing club, then under the leadership of Russ Ladkin. I wanted my first event to be the Hebridean Challenge, a five-day stage race in a team of five involving fell running, road cycling, mountain biking, kayaking and swimming, while navigating. Russ suggested I might want to start with a shorter day race. That was a reasonable suggestion, of course, but it only provoked me. If Russ wasn't going to let me join his team, then I'd find my own.

So my first adventure race was indeed 'The Heb', completed with my friend Lindsey and three Scotsmen we'd never met before. Although on paper it didn't seem we'd done too well (and indeed we were beaten by Russ's team), I think for an inexperienced group it was an impressive effort just to have finished the course. It was also a huge amount of fun, and from that one experience I became an adventure-racing addict.

I also discovered I was asthmatic – or rather, Lindsey did. We'd been friends for a long time, meeting at Guildford High School and both going to Charterhouse. Like me, Lindsey was academic but loved sport, despite not being great at it. While I'd been in Ghana she'd been volunteering in Malawi. Then she'd gone to Cambridge to study medicine. So perhaps it's no surprise she made the discovery. It happened in the race's prologue when, despite everyone knowing the race was not a sprint but a five-day slog, we all went 'balls out' as fast as we could. The prologue was a short relay and my leg started at the bottom and finished at the top of a hill. I arrived gasping for air and handed the baton to Lindsey, only instead of instantly running off, she remained where she was and stared at me.

'Go!' I gasped.

'You're having an asthma attack!' she replied.

'What? No, I'm not. I'm just out of breath. I've just run up a big fucking hill and I'm really unfit. Go!'

'Are you sure you're okay?'

'Yes! Now go!'

I was quite cross that all my effort had been wasted on that pointless exchange, but by the time I had walked back down the hill it had gone from my mind.

The next leg of the race was another relay, an individual thirty-kilometre cycling time trial. I was tagged by one of the boys and set off cycling hard, but then disgraced myself as I turned into the car park at the end of my leg, tagging one of the lads and forgetting I was attached to the bike. It was the first time I'd used clip-in pedals. Before I could figure out what to do, I toppled over on to the ground. At least I made everyone laugh.

Despite my faux pas, I was nominated to ride another road-cycling section as the boys were getting tired and I wanted to do as much of the race as I could. The leg culminated with a steep ascent and as I summited, my larynx went into spasm. Gasping for air, I held on to the large marshal to stop myself from crashing off the bike. The spasms didn't last too long, but they shocked me because such a thing had never happened to me before. Perhaps Lindsey was right. Maybe I did have a problem.

As a kid, I'd rarely been ill. I'd never missed a day at school, except when my mother sent me off with chickenpox. The school called her, saying she had to pick me up. My mother was a dedicated smoker and used to smoke in the house when we were kids. I remember drawing a sign that read 'No Smoking!' when I was seven or so and sticking it on my bedroom door. Not long after that, I smelled smoke in my bedroom and got so mad that I stole her cigarettes and threw them all away. I got into so much trouble, but I suppose it's possible her smoking contributed in some way to my asthma.

On a day-to-day basis I never had any trouble breathing; it was only when I really exerted myself that my chest would feel tight. I'd wheeze a lot and have long bouts of coughing. If this happened while I was running or cycling, the natural thing to do was to slow down. Normally this would ease most of my symptoms, but naturally it would cost me a few positions if I was racing. When I began to realise it was affecting my performance, I wondered if I should do something about it, even though I felt somewhat guilty about presenting myself to a doctor when I wasn't really ill. I recall a running camp in Cornwall with the Cambridge Hare and Hounds one summer. For the first time, I experienced an asthma attack at rest. Shortly after we arrived at our accommodation, I felt my chest tighten and my breathing rate increased. I found it hard to walk around and couldn't think about running, but after a day or two it settled and I continued as normal. I still didn't seek medical advice.

It wasn't until 2010, when I started having coughing bouts every morning and bringing up phlegm, that I decided to go and see the GP. I was lucky. I landed on a keen cyclist who had pedalled LEJOG (Land's End to John o'Groats). He assured me I wasn't wasting his time and we should be able to resolve my symptoms to the point where I could run or cycle fast enough that it was my legs getting tired and slowing me down, rather than my lungs not working properly. He put me on a medication called Montelukast, which reduces lung inflammation and relaxes smooth muscle. I was also prescribed a combined inhaler, Seretide, containing a bronchodilator that lasts around twelve hours and a corticosteroid that acts locally on the lungs to reduce inflammation. I felt so empowered and at the same time chastised myself for not having gone to see someone sooner. I certainly noticed an improvement in my health within a few days of starting the medication, the most noticeable being the reduction in morning phlegm and coughing. It was a bit longer before I noticed an improvement in breathing while running. However, my biggest problem, one I still struggle to overcome, is the lifelong habit I'd formed of controlling my speed to prevent the onset of breathing issues. Even now, I find it hard to push my top-end pace. I still don't know how much of this is psychological, or whether if I pushed myself too hard trying to sprint I might cause an asthma attack, despite my medication. Whichever it is, I prefer to run at a comfortable pace and I've never been keen on zone-four training, when you push your heart rate to ninety per cent of maximum, so I generally don't try to go too fast.

Sport gave me a lot of things, including a husband. I met Ben in a swimming pool in Cambridge. He'd noticed my strong swimming and asked what I was training for. I explained that I was a triathlete but that I also did adventure racing. Ben told me he had just started to get into triathlons too and wanted to know more about adventure racing. He was already a strong swimmer and biker but not so quick on the run, probably because he was well built. He had massive shoulder muscles from white-water kayaking, his main thing then: a risky sport but he was good at it. He was also into mountain biking, both cross-country and downhill. I kicked myself when I left without giving him my number.

A few weeks later, my heart raced a little when I saw an email from Ben in my inbox. It turned out Russ had put my email address on the CamRacers website. Thanks, Russ. Ben started coming along to some of our adventure-racing sessions and after learning how Air France had destroyed my mountain bike on the way back from a race in Turkey, offered to fix it. I was very impressed with his skills. He bent my disc brakes back into shape, trued up my wheels and my bike was as good as new. The rest is history.

In 2009 I graduated from vet school and started my first job in Leighton Buzzard in a mixed animal practice, meaning I dealt with all species: horses, cows, sheep, pigs, cats, dogs, ferrets and rabbits, to name only the most common. In those days (and it's not exactly that long ago) it was not unusual for newly graduated vets to work sixty- to eighty-hour weeks. I would work routine hours Monday to Friday: 9 a.m. to 7 p.m., occasion-ally getting to finish at 5 p.m. Then I'd spend one night a week on call, plus one in four weekends. The weekends were crazy. The evenings until about midnight would be filled with appointments for pets, and then the early hours with farm work, typically a cow caesarean at 5 a.m. During the day at weekends I'd often be tending to a lame or colicky horse. In addition to the large-animal emergencies, I'd simultaneously be trying to manage an inpatient cat or dog that was on a drip, or returning to the practice to perform surgery.

If you calculated my hourly rate, I wasn't even making minimum wage, but despite being overworked and underpaid, I really enjoyed it. I developed a greater interest in the small-animal emergency work, fixing animals with life-threatening conditions, something I found not only thrilling but extremely rewarding. Although I had originally wanted to be a vet so I could work outdoors, I found this emergency work much more engaging than the equine work, which was always quite repetitive (lameness, trauma, colic). And unless you wanted to work at an equine hospital, you never got to do surgery.

It was lucky for me that Ben was tolerant of my long working hours. Sometimes he would come with me and help. On Christmas Day 2009 we were invited to my boss's house for lunch as I was on call. On our way to his house, we had to call into the practice for an emergency. A little Patterdale terrier had eaten some rat poison the week before and had a serious bleeding issue. Unfortunately, he must have also eaten something sharp because the bleeding was in his throat and the large haematoma that had developed was causing an obstruction to his airways. He needed an emergency tracheostomy and there was no time to call anyone else for help. So, in our best clothes, we got to it. I anaesthetised the dog and placed the life-saving airway in his throat as well as injecting the antidote to the poison. We never got our Christmas dinner, but I think Ben was just as pleased as I was that we had together saved that little dog's life.

After two years, I decided to continue with small animals and give up the large-animal work. I took a postgraduate course in small-animal emergency medicine and surgery. I also took on locum night shifts in twenty-four-hour animal hospitals to gain more experience in emergency work. I'd often clock up eighty-hour weeks with little sleep. I'd never been good at sleeping anyway. Then I landed a dream job doing emergency work one week on and one week off. This was perfect. I'd work an intense week of night shifts, getting out for a run or cycle during the day, and then have a week off to train, go abroad for an adventure or do an extra week of work. Life was very busy and I didn't waste a moment.

I raced all over the world in various mixed teams: English, French, Irish and Spanish. The latter gave me a chance to practise my Spanish, which I'd picked up on my travels in Peru. Most teams were formed of one woman and three men, as they had to be mixed to be in the most competitive category. I was a sought-after teammate, being one of only a few women capable of running, biking and kayaking with an appetite for endurance sports and adventure. I started out as a strong cyclist and a relatively weak runner, but over the years that turned on its head. I found myself becoming stronger and stronger on the foot sections and more confident with navigating trails and rough terrain. In fact, I really began to enjoy that aspect.

By then, Ben and I were making frequent trips up to the Lake District to get our fill of mountain running. Through the years we've been together, we have both developed our running skills. Ben has always been and will always be faster than me at the short stuff. But once the distance exceeds ten kilometres, I can start to challenge him. He's never too bothered about beating me; he can be competitive, but only if he's in the right mood. When we raced mountain marathons together, he would set off fast, carrying both our packs while I was puffing along, struggling to keep up. An hour into it he would give me my pack back, and then a few hours later I'd be carrying his. I'd get frustrated that he would run out of steam and I'd be impatient and irritated when he wanted to sit down for a rest. I always felt like he was doing it on purpose, not trying, when actually he was tired and I couldn't understand that because I wasn't at all. In my head, he was faster and stronger than me and it would annoy me so much because we would often be winning, only to lose our position by dragging ourselves to the finish instead of maintaining pace.

My interest in mountain running grew to the point that I thought I would have a go at the Bob Graham Round, the legendary fell-running challenge that takes in forty-two of the highest Lakeland peaks across sixty-six miles and with 27,000 feet of ascent, all of it completed inside twenty-four hours. In August 2013 I planned my first go at the Bob Graham. We weren't living in the Lake District at that time but I had spent a lot of weekends in the mountains, sometimes supporting friends on their successful rounds. I finally felt ready to try this immense challenge and emailed lots of my adventure-racing friends, asking them to come out and support me. 'The weather forecast is not looking great, but with a little luck and a lot of help from my lovely friends I'll get round. A massive thank you to my amazing support team.' I also added a tracker link so they could follow my progress. 'Fingers crossed for the weather!'

Despite the crossed fingers, the weather did not come good. The next day I was writing another email. 'It's a shame I had to pull out at Honister, just before the short home leg. I really thought I had nailed it at Wasdale, even though I had been slowed down by the weather already. But once I'd started the fourth leg and climbed all the way up over Yewbarrow it was clear that the winds were just not ceasing. I had hoped that they would drop around lunchtime like the weather forecast said, but it just seemed to be getting worse.'

The first leg had been great fun. I found the sensible route off Blencathra, which meant I knocked an hour off my recce time. Ben and our friend Ant did a great job navigating through thick cloud. Leg two started with a bit of a hiccup. The tracker showed me running off round Threlkeld as I looked in vain for my support vehicles, not realising they were on the other side of the road. But I was twenty-five minutes up heading up Clough Head and, thanks to more incredible navigation in thick cloud from my new support runner, Mike, I managed not to lose any time on this section and arrived at Dunmail twenty-five minutes early.

On the third leg my legs started to feel a little heavy, but my feet were in good condition and I'd been eating well. Then we were submerged in more thick cloud for most of the leg, meaning we had to rely on a GPS tracker to know we were hitting the tops. We lost a little time on Harrison Stickle climbing up the wrong bit, then got slightly confused on Rossett Pike, never quite sure which bit was the top, but made back a bit of time going up to Bow Fell. Here the winds started to pick up and the rain began. It was challenging just to stay upright on the boulders and slippery rocks over Esk Pike, Great End, Ill Crag and Broad Crag. The wind was thrashing the rain into our faces as though someone were pelting us with stone. Still, I was quite happy knowing I was bang on schedule despite everything. Scafell Pike seemed relatively easy and we even saw some other crazy hikers out doing the Three Peaks. We knew we'd beat them to Wasdale, even with our diversion via Foxes Tarn and Scafell. Jeff, my running partner at that point, found the perfect route off Scafell, down scree to the grassy bit and the final descent into Wasdale. In the valley all seemed quite calm and bright, and there was no wind. It was 9 a.m. and I was bang on schedule, ready to tackle the next section.

The fourth leg turned out to be hell on earth. On a normal day, climbing

Yewbarrow would be the worst bit, but my new companions, Joe and Dave, kept me going at a good steady pace and I was surprised to hit the peak on schedule. However, once on the tops we were again lashed by the wind and rain. I had to hang on to Dave the whole way to stop myself flying around like a kite. It was hard work and we couldn't even take our minds off it by chatting. We couldn't hear a thing over the howling wind. Despite my being soaked to the skin, my Páramo jacket was still keeping me warm, but at this stage I was struggling to eat. Each peak was taking a little longer to reach and my time was ebbing away. We made up a bit here and there on the flatter bits, but it was clear that the twenty-four-hour mark was slowly creeping away. With that in mind, I couldn't put us through any more of the dreadful conditions. The deciding point came as I struggled to reach the cairn on top of Kirk Fell, being blown back by a forceful wind each time I approached, before an intense gust picked us up and dumped us back down, landing me on my back on a rock and breaking Dave's pole.

I wasn't as disappointed as I thought I would be. I felt from the outset that unless the forecast was wrong it was going to be mission impossible. The first eleven hours were actually quite blissful, navigationally challenging because we were in the clouds but in still conditions. But, apart from regret at the atrocious weather later on, in hindsight I feel I missed the point. Looking back at my report of the attempt almost a decade later, I realise I wasn't navigationally ready. The Bob Graham Round is not an ultra or a race: it is not a marked or prescribed route. Finding those forty-two named summits is a navigational challenge.

Navigation, for me, is making my way across the landscape in an efficient way using a map, a GPS device, people, route knowledge and experience to best negotiate any obstacles along the way: mountains, valleys, technical terrain, crags and rivers. This normally results in a route that deviates from a straight line between A and B. I particularly enjoyed this aspect of racing in mountain marathons. I loved that you could pick up a map without knowing an area and plan a route on or off paths to minimise distance travelled and height gained and lost from one checkpoint to another. Yet I enjoy even more the spontaneous changes to that route that you have to make on the fly, when you can actually see terrain that is not obvious on the map. For example, what might look like a well-established bridleway on the map might turn out to be a slow route due to boggy ground where the path disappears into mud and moss.

'I feel surprisingly good this morning,' I wrote to my supporters. 'Not too stiff. Feet are still in good nick. I'm quite hungry, though! I'm sure the BGR has not seen the last of me, but I will wait until I have moved up here before trying it again so that I can pick my day of good weather.'

It was ironic that at the time of planning my first Bob I had no idea that a few weeks later we'd be living at the heart of the route. When Ben and I met, one of the many things we had in common was a desire to live in the Lake District, but I hadn't expected it to happen so soon. In typical Sabs style, I put our house on the market, explaining to Ben that if it sold it would be fate and we should move to the Lake District. It sold within two weeks. I went online and made a search area, putting in the maximum amount we could afford. I shortlisted the houses that I thought were acceptable and then gave the list to Ben to shortlist further. We ended up with a list of thirty houses and I arranged to view all of them over two days. We drove to the Lake District and had about fifteen minutes to view each property. Sometimes we didn't even bother to go inside as the location or something outside the property put us off; the estate agents didn't know what had hit them. After that we had a shortlist of three.

We made our choice and a few months later had bought our house and the Great Langdale Bunkhouse that came with it. Ben would manage the bunkhouse while I continued my veterinary work down south on a rota of one week on and two weeks off. The dream was eventually to open our own veterinary practice in the Lake District. In September 2013, a month after my first attempt on the Bob Graham Round, Ben and I had swapped the flatlands of Bedfordshire for beautiful, mountainous Cumbria. From our new front door I would have direct access to the fells: the Langdale Pikes to the north, Bow Fell and Scafell Pike to the west and Lingmoor Fell to the south. As we drove into Langdale, passing over the cattle grid at Elterwater just as the magnificent Langdale Pikes came into view, I knew we had made the right decision.

THREE
GOING THE DISTANCE

The first time I heard about the Wainwright summits challenge was from Steve Birkinshaw. I had met him a few times at races and admired him from afar as a gifted orienteer and speedy mountain marathoner, and I knew he had also adventure-raced. In May 2014 I got a message from him about the logistics for his Wainwright run. What is a Wainwright? A Wainwright refers to one of the 214 peaks Alfred Wainwright described and depicted in his famous guidebooks to the Lakeland Fells. Steve wanted to run them all in a continuous round as fast as possible.

'Are you still happy for me to use your Great Langdale Bunkhouse as a bit of a base? I am due there on Monday 16 June at 11 a.m. but I could be quite a few hours in front or behind that schedule.'

I was flattered Steve had contacted me and more than happy for him to use the bunkhouse. He could have the house, for that matter. But I was also annoyed to be working that week. I would have to follow his progress on my phone, 'dot watching' from Surrey while Ben got to be a part of Steve's big adventure. I was also intrigued by the challenge and, after watching how Steve did it, I felt it was something I'd like to try. I thought of it as a challenge where I could put my adventure-racing skills to good use. I would aim to do it in 2020, before I turned forty. Little did I know at this stage that running around all the Wainwrights would become an obsession.

I had really enjoyed adventure racing. It was fun to explore different parts of the world while doing different sports (running, biking, kayaking, 'coasteering', rock climbing, abseiling, caving) in teams from different cultures. And it was fun getting to know different teammates. I felt I was getting stronger and would have liked to make the podium in the Adventure Racing World Championships. I had raced in the Worlds a few times: Portugal in 2009, Costa Rica in 2013, Australia in 2016. And I raced with lots of different teams. But over the years it became apparent that the rest of the team couldn't keep up with me on the longer trekking stages. That started me thinking about racing ultras on my own; it was that thought process kicking into action when I watched Steve complete the Wainwrights. This was a challenge I would enjoy: the navigation, the running, the fells, managing my time efficiently at support points and managing my body through the long journey. It really appealed. So I decided to enter my first ultra, the Grand Tour of Skiddaw.

I loved everything about this race, particularly the fact I could turn up a few minutes before the start and there was only a small field of people racing, fewer than 200. I had read all the rules and packed a support-point bag as requested, filling it with useful things, just as I would for an adventure race: spare socks, spare shoes, extra layers, a fresh waterproof, waterproof trousers, extra food, spare warm layers. When I handed it in at registration I was given a bit of stick for how large it was, and in fact won a prize for the person with the biggest support bag. I was embarrassed, but so inexperienced that I had no idea how long forty-four miles of mountain running was going to take me. It became apparent how ridiculous this was when I arrived at the support point in under five hours and didn't even open my bag. I was shocked to be the first woman to cross the finish line and fifth overall.

The race confirmed my hunch that ultrarunning was my sort of thing and that I was going to be good at it. I continued to adventure-race but gradually found myself becoming addicted to ultras. I learnt about the Ultra-Trail du Mont-Blanc (UTMB) and how other runners were entering races to collect qualification points. This seemed to be the natural way to progress, so without thinking about it I looked up those qualifying races and realised that in order to run the UTMB I would need to race a 100-miler. And if I wanted to race in the UTMB the following year, I would need to do that before the end of the current year. So I found the only race I could do and entered it. Having raced in only one ultra, I flew off that December to Poland for the 147-kilometre Łemkowyna Ultra-Trail.

It was exciting to go and race in another country; the organisers were so welcoming and made the process easy for me. They even offered me the chance to bring someone for free, so I invited my childhood friend Lindsey. She was used to accompanying me on my mad escapades but sensibly resisted the long race, instead entering the thirty-kilometre trail race which took place at the same time. As I stood on the start line, another runner turned to me.

'What's your plan?'

I didn't have a plan for the race. My plan had been focused on the harder task of getting to the start line. Now I was there, all I had to do was run, right?

Things actually went well until about halfway through, when I started to feel a bit of pain in one of my knees. It had snowed for some of the race and conditions were very cold through the early hours of the morning when finishing. I also suffered an asthma attack. Yet I still finished first female and eighteenth overall. Not bad, I thought, for a first long ultra. That night I suffered an uncomfortably high respiratory rate and woke in the night wheezing and coughing, choking on my own sputum. Luckily, Lindsey was there to give me life-saving back slaps to dislodge it. And by morning my little knee injury had turned into a big swollen problem that was later diagnosed as prepatellar bursitis. With Lindsey's help, I managed to hobble on to the bus and through the airport to make it home.

Despite that minor setback, three weeks later the injury had healed and I was back running and even more enthused. I had all the UTMB points I needed but didn't enter in the end, as my calendar was already full with adventure races. Adventure racing was going well and I had been asked to compete with some good teams, including a French and then a Spanish group. Yet, despite this success, I had started to grow tired of the déjà-vu

WHERE THERE'S A HILL

experience of racing with three men who treated me as though I was there to be seen but not to speak my mind. Despite me having far more experience than the men inviting me to race with them, their idea of my contribution to the team was simply to fulfil the female requirement. All championship races require mixed teams, meaning at least one male and one female. There are some successful teams that race with two women and two men, and a few with three women and one man, but generally it's three men and one woman.

I always found that on the first day of multi-day races I would be working extremely hard, forced into an anaerobic level of exercise I found uncomfortable. As a consequence, I often struggled to keep up. Come day two, however, the opposite was true. While I had been happy to push hard and just try to keep up on the first day, when my breathing slowed on day two I found the pace easy and so wanted to be a more productive member of the team, in whatever way I could help. I enjoy logistics and map reading but it was clear the guys had no interest in letting a woman do these things. I often found that after twenty-four hours or more without sleep, the guys would really suffer and start making silly mistakes while I felt my mind was still working well. So I noticed when we were going the wrong way or when our strategy was not optimal. Yet if I dared to speak up and say anything, it would either get brushed off or end up in an argument I would always lose.

In the Australian World Championships in 2016, I was racing with a Spanish team. We had done well for the first three days and were well up in the top twenty. Then we faced a long kayaking stage lasting a day and a night. I had asked the rest of the team to pack their warm neoprene layers for this section but they had ignored me. I paddled in mine the whole time so when the temparature dropped during the night I was already toasty warm while they got cold. When we finally reached the next transition, swapping kayaks for bikes, it was still dark. So I suggested we sleep at the support point, since it was clear they were all a bit slow and inefficient with sleep deprivation and cold. A place where we had access to warm kit and where it was dark was a good place to sleep. My suggestion was ignored. We headed straight out on our mountain bikes.

28

I had marked up the maps for this section before the race started and knew navigation was really simple. Something like: 'cycle east on a road for fifteen kilometres and then turn south and head down the road for another fifteen kilometres.' So, despite not being allowed to have a map in my hand, I knew we were going the wrong way when our navigator took us down a single track. I became frustrated. Not only did I know we were going the wrong way but the trail was also difficult to cycle. There were all sorts of hazards, like giant spiders and their huge webs spanning a metre across the track.

I pleaded with my teammates for ages to at least give me the other set of maps so that I could second their navigator, especially as no one was using them anyway. They didn't want to stop and get them out, preferring instead to continue on the pointless mission deeper and deeper into the under-growth. Eventually, after an hour or so, the narrow track petered out altogether and the navigator conceded he was lost. After another hour we arrived back at the transition. Once again I suggested that perhaps we should all have a sleep so that the navigator was refreshed for the next stage. They still wouldn't rest.

At least we were cycling on the road and I felt a bit more confident we were going the right way. Then, after only twenty minutes or so, one of my teammates fell asleep on his bike and fell off. Luckily, he wasn't badly injured, just a bit bruised and shocked. I hoped it might have woken him up a little. Once again the navigator started doing strange things. He kept trying to turn off the road where there weren't any turnings. He still wouldn't give up the maps, but at least I had managed to grab the second set out of another teammate's bag.

The next few hours were unbearably tedious. We were cycling more and more slowly and wasting more and more time turning off the road in random directions. I knew the team were sleep-deprived and barely func-tioning. Now I had the maps, I was managing to keep us on track, but despite my confident navigation, my teammates couldn't keep up the pace behind me, and when daylight eventually arrived they conceded they were tired and wanted to sleep. So in broad daylight we slept for two hours while half a dozen teams overtook us. I saw our chance at a good position slipping away, frustrated that we were wasting precious daylight sleeping after struggling through the night.

I decided at that moment to never race again with that team or any team that wasn't going to treat me with respect and as an equal. I also decided I would be happier on my own, ultrarunning. I could compete to the best of my ability without being hampered by teammates who thought I was useless.

I became a good adventure racer because I had a natural aptitude for endurance and self-reliance. From the start I dealt well with sleep deprivation, and by the end I was an expert. Sleep deprivation affects everyone differently. Some people have a greater tolerance than others for lack of sleep. I would say the most important thing is to find out what your own personal tolerance is and what happens to you when you're tired. Can you still function mentally and physically? I experienced sleep deprivation many times and learnt the hard way how to manage myself, whether I should rest or continue. Sleep deprivation can feel like torture. The experience makes you want to give in to your body's overwhelming desire to curl up and go to sleep anywhere: in the grass, in a ditch, on the road. If I'm racing hard, the adrenaline helps to overcome this, but when the momentum of the team drops and it seems like you're just plodding along, you really start to feel it. Then my eyelids start to feel really heavy and I find it so hard to fight against their weight; I think about wedging matchsticks in to keep them open. Your tired brain tries to make sense of the world around you, but it's misfiring and doing strange things, for example imagining that everything around you is alive. You're hallucinating.

In 2013, at the World Championships in Costa Rica, I suffered the worst case of sleep deprivation I've ever had. We had missed a cut-off time, one I knew we could have made if the team had wanted it, and ended up on a bus to rejoin the race. As soon as we got on board, my mind gave up on the race. I didn't want it any more because we weren't going to finish the long course. My body went into repair mode. When we got off the bus and started cycling, I had lost the plot. My poor teammates. I'd cycle along the road for a bit and then give in to my fatigue. My mind kept playing tricks on me. I kept turning into a hedge because I thought it was a garage where

I could park my bike. The wheel would get lodged in the hedge and I would fall asleep. Meanwhile, the rest of the team had gone ahead before eventually realising I wasn't with them. They tried everything to snap me out of it, but I was beyond help.

My mental state became even worse when we got lost in a banana plantation. It felt like we were going round and round in circles forever, and whenever their eyes were off me I curled up into a ball on the ground and went to sleep. Finally, after they had left me for twenty minutes, I woke up feeling sprightlier, but something had definitely gone wrong upstairs. I was convinced I knew the way to the finish. I explained the route was up the hill and through the farm where there was a tap we could use to fill our water bottles. Given they knew I'd never been to Costa Rica before, it was clear I'd gone nuts. Some long hours later we crossed the finish line, quite happy and still friends.

I learnt a valuable lesson that day. If I wanted to race well to the finish, I would have to stay focused. I have often watched teammates battling with sleep demons and have tried various things to snap them out of it: something sugary to eat, a caffeine drink, talking to them, increasing our focus and speed. Something would normally work, but once none of these things worked then sleep was the only thing that would. I employed these strategies on myself as well. I knew my teammates were too tired to look out for me. Every time I drifted off, I'd go through the motions: eat something, drink something, have some caffeine, talk to people, refocus and push the pace. Focusing on the race was important. The minute it seemed the team weren't up for doing the best we could and pushing hard, I was no longer interested.

When the clock is ticking in these non-stop races it becomes a question of balancing 'moving time' against 'resting time'. It's actually quite hard to catch up on time you lose sleeping. If you race for twenty-four hours and spend eight of them asleep, you might feel sufficiently rested to run a bit faster but no one could make up that sort of delay. If your average moving speed is six kilometres per hour and you don't sleep, then you cover 144 kilometres. If you sleep for eight hours you are only moving for sixteen and consequently have to run an average of nine kilometres an hour to go the same distance. That's fifty per cent faster. Having said that, there is obviously a point or a limit you reach where your speed slows and you cannot maintain those six kilometres an hour. At this point it is beneficial to have a rest. For me, I can normally manage the first night without sleep and still move at a reasonable speed as well as function mentally.

When I wrote the schedule for my first Wainwrights attempt, I planned to have my first sleep after forty-eight hours. By then I expected to be back at Langdale and so able to sleep in my own bed. (I'd been forced to plan things that way because of Covid-19 and didn't yet have access to a camper van.) I didn't make it that far on the first try, but I did on the second and I remember how that final leg into Langdale took forever because I was too sleep-deprived. I couldn't keep my eyes open. I found it hard to focus and keep moving forward when all I wanted to do was curl up on the ground and sleep. It would certainly have been better to sleep a little earlier. So when I wrote the schedule for my third attempt, I timed my first sleep at about forty hours after starting. That made a big difference. Sleeping in the first part of the second night rather than the latter part was much more efficient for me. An hour and a half asleep meant I woke up refreshed, as though I had enjoyed a whole night's sleep. For the fourth and successful attempt I kept this sleeping strategy and it worked very well. I only had a couple of moments on the hill when I felt too sleepy to continue and took a two-minute 'power nap' which sufficed to get me to the next support point.

Between 2014 and 2016 I continued with adventure racing while at the same time pushing my ultrarunning experience. In 2015 I decided to enter the legendary Dragon's Back Race: five days running and navigating over the hills of Wales sounded great fun. Despite never having run 320 kilometres, I was confident that I would enjoy it and thought finishing would be a good test of my progress. I didn't worry about the pitfalls or whether I could run that far. I didn't question if I was ready or capable. I just showed up and gave it a go.

The 2015 Dragon's Back was very different from the 2021 race. We were only given the route at registration and there were no GPX files for our watches; it made for a true navigational challenge. I had not recced any of the route in order not to spoil the surprise. The only part I knew was the Welsh 3,000ers because a friend had once asked me to run this challenge with them. And that had been in the opposite direction to how we would do it in the race.

With fewer than 200 starters, it was a small race but with a very high calibre of runners: Jasmin Paris, her husband Konrad Rawlik, Jim Mann, Beth Pascall, Joasia Zakrzewski, Lizzie Wraith, Jez Bragg, Damian Hall, Pavel Paloncy and Charlie Sharpe. I was very flattered that Helen Diamantides, paired winner with Martin Stone in the 1992 race, picked me (a nobody) out of the crowd and said she thought I would finish. And I did. The race was tough but I was inspired by those around me, particularly the strong field of women who were just as fast as the men. I revelled in the navigation, especially when I discovered that my route choices allowed me to climb the rankings, something I might not have achieved on my running speed alone.

I was the fifth woman to finish and fourteenth overall, which I was very pleased with. In fact, I enjoyed it so much I didn't hesitate to commit myself to race it again when it was next held two years later and again in 2019. Through those years my running was improving, which was reflected in my times on day one, the easiest leg to compare because the route remains consistently the same, unlike the other stages. In 2015 my time and position (ladies and overall) for the first day of the Dragon's Back were ten hours, thirty-six minutes and eight seconds and fifth/fourteenth. In 2017 my time had improved to nine hours, twenty-seven minutes and two seconds and my position to second/thirteenth. My performance in 2019 was even better: nine hours, ten minutes and twenty seconds and placing second/twenty-first. My time for day one had fallen by eighty-six minutes between 2015 and 2019.

During these years I still had my eye firmly on the ultimate prize: the Wainwrights. However, the more I raced, the more aware I became of my strengths and weaknesses. It was clear that my descending skills were good, especially down non-technical terrain, and my strong quads did not fatigue or give me delayed-onset muscle soreness (DOMS), but I was by comparison poor at climbing. I noticed this particularly in the 2019 Dragon's Back. Climbing up, I was overtaken by runners I was quicker than overall, because when it came to the downhill I'd come thundering past. Before I could tackle the Wainwrights, I knew I would have to improve this aspect. And what better way to get stronger than doing recces?

The 2019 racing season was a busy one, perhaps too busy. March was the Lakes Mountain 42. In April I ran the Coledale Horseshoe, then two Yorkshire races, the Calderdale Hike and The Fellsman. That May I was back in Wales for the Dragon's Back and then Scotland for the Ramsay Round. In June it was the Lakeland Five Passes and the Summer Spine Race, racing up the Pennine Way. July meant the Saunders Mountain Marathon and the Lakeland 100.

I knew I'd done too much. I remember standing on the start line of the Spine Race feeling that my legs had not recovered from the Dragon's Back, followed two weeks later with a Ramsay Round recce (twenty-six hours) and then a thirty-five-mile ultra the week after. How did I end up doing so much racing? It certainly wasn't planned. The Ramsay Round was my own doing – a sudden urge for a weekend of running and the right weather window. Karen Nash was responsible for guilt-tripping me into completing the Runfurther race series, hence the Lakeland Five Passes. (This was so I would win the trophy instead of Karen, which, as the organiser, was getting embarrassing for her.) I had entered the Summer Spine after I knew I had a place in the Lakeland 100 and had been willing to sacrifice one for the other.

While I was racing in the Lakes Five Passes, Paul Tierney set off on his record-breaking Wainwrights run. The day after my race, I was supposed to run with him on part of the leg out of Langdale. But I'd fallen over in the ultra and bashed my knee, which had swollen so much I could barely walk. I was annoyed at myself; I couldn't help Paul and I had also jeopardised my Summer Spine Race. I didn't even start to pack my Spine bag until the day before leaving for Edale as I hadn't been convinced I was going to start. However, standing on the line with tired legs, I decided to begin slowly and see how I got on. And I promised my body that afterwards I would give it a good rest.

To my surprise, I nailed it. I raced consistently well along the Pennine Way and finished first overall. I was over the moon. It was the first long ultra that I had done that wasn't a stage race and I had really enjoyed it. I loved it so much because it was exactly what I had wanted: a solo adventure race on foot. I had enjoyed the navigation, the looking after myself, finding water, making sure I ate well, managing my kit and my sleep. All of it. I had been very efficient in the transitions and kept my time in them down to a minimum. Most of all I absolutely loved the support and kindness of the Spine family.

I don't remember too much about the start of the race. The first real memory I have is catching sight of the two frontrunners on the approach to Stoodley Pike. I chastised myself for catching them up too quickly because I knew if I was in front early on I could well end up racing on my own for the next four days. I tried to slow down, but even then I gained ground. So the three of us – Cees van der Land, Esteban Diaz and me – trotted on to Hebden together. The transition was amusing. I took five minutes to change my socks, eat some food and pack my bag. I was about to walk out the door when the other two looked up in shock. Cees quickly pulled his shoes on and chased after me so I wouldn't get away. I remember thinking that I hoped he hadn't forgotten to do something important in his panic, but at the same time I was very glad of the company.

I knew my ability to be efficient at the support points would be a strength, wasting no time, along with my ability to focus on my own race. I'd never have changed what I was doing because another racer overtook me; I would stick to my own plan. Cees and I continued together along the Pennine Way, making conversation. I enjoyed his company, apart from his poles, which kept stabbing me in the heel. I have to admit to telling him, grumpily, that if he wanted to come with me he would have to ditch them at Hawes, the next support point some forty kilometres away. And he did.

Just after Horton, about twenty kilometres before Hawes, Cees began feeling weary and vomited. I discovered the only trail food he had was gels. He sat down by a little beck at Birkwith Moor and said he needed to sleep. I made him eat some of my cheese and crackers and get all his layers on so he wouldn't get cold. I didn't really want to leave him there because it would be more fun trotting along with him, but he knew what he needed. I also knew that I needed to keep moving and that Hawes was not too far away. So we said our goodbyes and I trotted off, leading the race but hoping he would catch me up because there were still 170 miles to go.

I remember getting into Hawes village and being a little disoriented with the roads. Unlike the fell, where you can just follow a compass direction, you can't just walk through buildings that are in your path to get back on the Pennine Way. I felt weary and also hungry so I stopped in a cafe and ordered a cheese toastie. If I'd known how long it was going to take I wouldn't have bothered. When I finally pulled into the support point on the far side of Hawes, Cees was already there, tucking into some food. He had overtaken me while I was in the cafe waiting for that toastie.

I was ready to leave in about five minutes but Cees wanted me to wait: he was having his feet taped. I'd never done this before and thought maybe I would give it a go as I had a couple of hotspots. The medics were very willing and got to work. It took them a surprisingly long time as they insisted on cutting the right shape and so on; I have to admit to getting a little frustrated with all the faffing. At first the tape seemed to have been a great choice. My feet felt comfortable, like they were encased in sponge, but after some miles the tape started to annoy me.

By the top of Great Shunner Fell, third-highest hill in the Yorkshire Dales, I had forgotten about my feet entirely. It was clear Cees was able to run a bit faster than me but he was definitely sticking with me. I didn't know if that was because he felt guilty for making me wait for him, because he wanted company, or because he thought he needed me. Whatever the answer, it didn't really matter to me. I knew that at some point in this race I was going to end up on my own for a long time, so I might as well enjoy company while I had it.

On the way into Middleton, Cees told me he wanted to sleep there for four hours. I certainly didn't, and was annoyed that I found myself negotiating. I didn't want to stop for more than two hours, but I think we compromised on three. I was thinking to myself that I really ought to stick to my own race strategy, but felt a bit guilty knowing Cees needed more time there than I did and that he would run himself into the ground if I insisted on leaving earlier.

We asked the support team to be our wake-up call when it was time to leave and we both went to bed. I managed to sleep for about thirty minutes but then woke up. The central heating system had been turned on and I was roasting. Too awake to go back to sleep, I went downstairs to eat some food. I really wanted to get going again, but didn't want to leave without letting Cees know. I worried he might view it as a deceitful race tactic. So one of the support team went to tell him I was leaving so he had the option to come with me or carry on sleeping. He decided to come.

As we were about to leave, Esteban, currently second male and third overall, pulled in, looking very wet. It was nasty outside and the storm was due to continue for a few more hours. I put on another layer and my poncho on top of that. Cees and I then set off climbing up towards Cauldron Snout. It was getting colder and wetter, so I loaned Cees my other poncho as he seemed to be suffering. Morning arrived and it got a bit warmer. The rain stopped but it was still claggy. The tarmacked path to High Cup Nick was easy going, so Cees broke into a fast run, around ten kilometres an hour. There was no way I was going to chase that down, so I let him charge off into the mist and continued at my gentle trot.

I thought it was weird that I couldn't see Cees in the distance when I crossed the river, but he had been going very fast and it was still cloudy. I assumed he must have disappeared ahead. At High Cupgill Head I noticed the GPS trace had a little kink, almost suggesting I should go down, but that didn't make sense so I got the map out. No, I decided, definitely across the little stream and up on to High Cup Nick. After reaching the top of the path, I thundered down the descent. Feeling strong, I assumed I was bound to catch Cees at this pace. But with a clear view for a few kilometres ahead I still couldn't see him. *Wow*, I thought, *he really did crack on. Good for him.*

At Dufton, race director Scott Gilmour was asleep in his car. I was glad to see him and he was delighted to tell me that Cees was in fact behind me. I was confused.

'Oh well,' I said, 'tell him to get a shuffle on and catch me up.' Cees finally caught me near the top of Cross Fell. He had taken that wrong turn down High Cup Gill from High Cup Nick. He was pleased to see me and from that point on wasn't going to leave my side.

Running down into Garrigill along the cobbled path was quite punishing on bruised feet. It was daylight but we were both a little sleepy so we stopped to get a coffee from the local post office. It was a surreal experience as we sat at a table on the village green drinking coffee as though we were having a lazy start to the day. It wasn't far to Alston, where we were treated to some tasty Spine Race lasagne. Five minutes later, I was ready to leave but Cees hadn't got his shoes on. He was determined to stick with me, so rushed himself to keep up. But only a few kilometres across some fields, Cees exclaimed he had the wrong shoes on. He was now clearly caught in a dilemma: leave me to get ahead or carry on with uncomfortable feet. He elected to go back and change and said he would catch me up. I walked on, trying not to rush. I didn't want to stop or go back, but I did want Cees to sort himself out and catch up. Amazingly, he did, around Slaggyford, where a sweet little girl and her father greeted us, handing us some treats to eat.

Over the next section, neither Cees nor I were going well. I think we'd run out of water and got ourselves a bit dehydrated, which was silly because we could have asked for some at the house at Slaggyford. I remember apologising to Cees as I had to stop every few minutes to try to wee and then none would come out. This worried me. When we finally did get some water, I really did need to stop every few minutes to wee. Looking back, I now understand that my kidneys were using that much-needed water to flush out all the toxins that had built up during the dry spell.

A bit further on, Cees mentioned that he had passed some black stools. Being a vet, I heard alarm bells ringing in my head. I told Cees they were likely black from digested blood and that meant he must have an internal bleed from a gastric or intestinal ulcer. We kept moving, but only slowly, discussing the problem for a bit. Then I texted the Spine Race safety team to tell them Cees would need to see a medic at the next opportunity, the village of Greenhead, west of Haltwhistle, about eight kilometres ahead of us.

The team rang back to ask the obvious question I hadn't dared broach with Cees: 'Should he continue racing?' I already knew the answer, but over the next kilometre I discussed the situation with Cees. He decided to ring his wife. We stopped and sat on a little patch of grass while he chatted to her. Luckily she was nearby in a car and made Cees realise there were more important things than finishing the race. We weren't going to make it to Greenhead, but instead staggered to the road junction just before what Spiners will recognise as the 'crazy Rasta man's house'. Cees's wife met us there, and later on Scott Gilmour joined us as well. I had been worried about Cees, but once he was in safe hands I felt I should press on. I had got so cold while we stopped, even with the sleeping bag Cees's wife lent me. I set off, wrapping my foil blanket around me like a skirt, ready to tackle the bogs of Blenkinsopp alone.

It felt different, running along on my own, but I soon adjusted to it. There was no safety net if I fell in a bog, no friendly hand to help with gates, no stimulating conversation, but there was no distraction from my mission. I was fully focused on the task in hand. I would put the hammer down and race hard to claim the Spine victory that was truly mine. It was a beautiful night on Hadrian's Wall, but I was a little scared of the cows that took umbrage at my head torch. I had to do all sorts of things to avoid having them charge me.

I had expected the safety team to provide a water refill point at The Sill but was disappointed. I had to press on for two more hours without anything to drink until Kevin McCann from the Spine team met me at Ladyhill. After Shitlington Crags I became rather disoriented. I think I must have fallen asleep on my feet because somehow I turned 180 degrees without knowing it. I then meticulously followed the Pennine Way on the map and my GPS track but in the wrong direction, unknowingly retracing my steps. I only realised what I'd done when for the second time I came across an odd bit of yellow piping that looked out of place on the open fell. Then the penny dropped. It was beyond frustrating, knowing that I had needlessly covered extra ground, but I was so close to my next planned stop at Bellingham, on the banks of the North Tyne, that I simply refocused.

Come on, Sabs. You've got this.

I slept at Bellingham for about ninety minutes to make sure I was able to cross the Cheviots sensibly. Then I was up on to Byrness Hill and into the clag across Houx Hill. Some people appeared from out of the mist.

'Are you doing the Pennine Way?' they asked.

'Yes. I'm running the Spine Race.' I didn't dare add that I was winning the Spine Race. Because surely I was in a dream and this wasn't real. *Focus, Sabs, let's get to Hut 2.*

I was imagining which exciting person or people were lying in wait for me in the shelter of Hut 2. This was the climax of the race: ten kilometres from the end of the Pennine Way at Kirk Yetholm and all downhill from there. The wind was really picking up and its full force was in my face but it felt good to me; it was refreshing and keeping me awake, and anyway I had so many layers on I was a good temperature. It seemed to be taking longer than I wanted but I was enjoying every minute of it. I could see Hut 1 but I knew there was no one in it. And although I was weary and could have done with a little sleep and some shelter from the wind, I had to push on. I couldn't lose focus. I had to finish the race. I was lucky it was daylight and I was loving the lush green grass. *Green means go. Go, Sabs. Go.*

I imagined the dot watchers on their sofas. I imagined them willing my dot along, willing the little dot to the border. I was having to fight the wind but I was powerful and I would get there. I saw a figure coming towards me. It was Chris from Hut 2. He yanked the hut door open and we scooted in before the wind slammed the door behind us. Chris and his mate made me a cup of tea but they didn't have any sugar so I dipped a dry cheese sandwich into it. Years later I met Chris again and he remembered me being grumpy about the lack of sugar. Being so badly sleep-deprived is like being drunk. You think you're behaving reasonably, but in fact are likely being obnoxious and rude. I'd like to apologise. I knew I needed some fuel for the last ten kilometres because I hadn't managed to eat much since Byrness. That was over six hours ago at the start of the Cheviots, some thirty kilometres away. *Right. I'm ready.* I thrust myself out into the ferocious wind, I scooted down The Schil, the last hill on the Cheviots, and there was nothing that could stop me thundering down the hill to victory.

I am the first finisher. I have won the Summer Spine Race.

FOUR

THE WRECKED AND THE DAMNED

After the Summer Spine Race, I did not keep my promise to my body. Against my better judgement, a fortnight later I raced at the Saunders Mountain Marathon with my husband. I had suggested we do the easiest class but Ben wanted a more challenging course. It was an epic fail in every way. I was tired and the terrain was brutal, contouring and uneven ground that strained my ankle and foot muscles and pained my tired legs. I knew I shouldn't race the Lakeland 100 in another two weeks. I knew I couldn't race to the best of my ability. Yet, even knowing all that, I suffered huge fear of missing out. I decided I would rather not finish than not start. I ran the sixty miles to Dalemain and decided to stop, even though I arrived leading the ladies' race. I knew it was just too much. After that I gave myself a good chunk of time off and took it easy.

At some point in this period of recovery, I reminded myself of the Wainwrights challenge. The year 2020 was rapidly approaching and I needed to start exploring the route. That process got underway in September 2019 when I headed to the Far Eastern Fells that I had not previously visited. I did a lot of the recces on my own: it was the most efficient way to use my time. I could plan where and how far I wanted to go and then just set off without much notice. The whole process excited me; I was going to new places I hadn't been before. I was map reading and had purpose to my running. I never tried to run fast during these journeys, but concentrated more on the route choice, the trods and how best to link the summits. I could go for hours and still feel frustrated when I had to turn back because I needed to be home or go back to work.

On these recces I needed my skills of self-sufficiency, making sure I ate enough food and drank enough water, took the right clothing and put it on before I got too cold and wet. I went out a lot that winter and got used to my head torch, making sure it was fully charged, taking spare batteries and changing them in the pitch black and poor weather conditions. I remember heading out for a long day to bag Shipman Knotts, Kentmere Pike, Tarn Crag, Grey Crag, Selside Pike, Branstree and Harter Fell, and then for no real reason other than the extra adventure choosing to circumnavigate Haweswater before returning via Mosedale. It was a soaking wet day and I went through all three pairs of gloves I'd brought with me, deciding none of them were waterproof as stated. I needed better gloves.

Sometimes I would find a friend to come and join me on my crazy escapades. Peter Sowerby was often a willing victim. With an ambition to do a Lakeland 100, Pete wanted to get fitter. We seemed always to have atrocious weather on these recces. One winter evening, we headed out from Langdale in the dark drizzle. I'd been my usual overambitious self and planned a route that we physically could not have completed in the given time. Nevertheless, we climbed up to Loft Crag in the last of the winter daylight. It was cold and wet, but we were suitably attired and had packs with spare layers and food. Ben and I had been invited out to dinner with some friends that evening but I'd had to turn it down because I was committed to the recce. While the cold rain lashed my face and my thighs burned as I pushed on up Tarn Crag, I pictured them all sat beside an open fire with a hearty meal in a cosy pub.

I enjoyed my recces with Pete. We would chat about all sorts of things: our work, our families, things that had happened in the news. But we were also perfectly comfortable walking or trotting along in silence for long periods of time. One of the best things about him was that, while Pete is a qualified mountain leader and has perfectly good navigational skills, he was happy to let me choose the route and navigate. He never once questioned where I was taking him or whether we were going the right way. Sometimes in the dark, claggy nights the navigation was challenging, and because the ground conditions were often boggy and slippery we ended up moving slowly. Often on these trips Pete would remark about what a huge undertaking doing the Wainwrights Round was. I couldn't disagree with him. Especially when my six-hour recce was rapidly turning into eight hours, despite missing out the last few summits.

In spite of this, I knew with the right weather and ground conditions and without having to carry a pack I would be able to move a lot faster. On these recces I tried to make a note of the time it took me between summits and when I got home I put them into a spreadsheet. I worked on the basis that with a heavy bag but fresh legs in winter, the time to do a section would be similar to doing it on tired legs in summer.

These recces also proved useful training for the Winter Spine Race. Running in the cold, dark and wet for prolonged periods was perfect for testing kit like head torches and waterproofs. Through November I continued my recces and building my hill fitness, but started loading my bag with more weight to get used to running with a heavy pack. Ben and I then went on our honeymoon to Everest, cannily before the actual wedding, which was planned for January 2020. I guess we wanted a good excuse for splashing out on a trip to Everest, so instead of having a proper honeymoon to a beach somewhere, Ben and I entered the Original Everest Marathon. The race involved hiking up in a group to base camp over two weeks to acclimatise, and then racing back down from 5,184 metres to Namche Bazaar at 3,446 metres. The trip was fun but it was incredibly cold: we were camping in temperatures of -15° Celsius with ice forming on the inside of our tents. A virus went round the group and I particularly suffered, from this and my asthma, which was triggered by the cold air. By race day my breathing was severely affected, but luckily there were not many uphill sections on the way down so I did manage to run some of it. By the time I reached the little airport at Lukla I had a high fever and was coughing non-stop. I remember feeling very unwell. We flew back to Kathmandu and I spent the three days before we headed home in bed. Back home, I was sick for another fortnight, either in bed or else working. Luckily I was on call and sleeping above the practice. I have since wondered if this was Covid-19, which was then emerging in China, but I suppose I'll never know.

By then, it was only three weeks before the Winter Spine Race and, having not run for a good few weeks, I was not in good shape. It's always amazing to see how quickly muscles can waste away when they are not used at all. I was still coughing but had started to get a little energy back. I did a couple of weeks of light running and knew I would have to rely on my base fitness to drag myself through the race. It wouldn't be a sterling performance but I hoped that I could at least complete the course.

At registration in Edale, after my victory in the summer event, people were expecting me not only to win the ladies' race but the whole thing. I didn't feel comfortable with that. I had turned up to have some fun and challenge myself to complete what's been dubbed 'Britain's most brutal race'. I felt bad knowing I was going to disappoint people, but I had my own expectations of myself: my goal was simply to finish the race.

I set off at a steady pace, not racing anyone. Then, about an hour in and in front of the race camera crew, I managed to trip and face-plant. I went down so hard that all the racers around stopped dead in their tracks to check I was okay. Embarrassed, I got up slowly and insisted they should run on and not worry. I felt guilty they would waste time on me, knowing that before too long I would likely come running past them. The fall had smarted; my knees were throbbing but I didn't dare look at them. Instead, I picked myself up and hobbled back into a trot. Kinder Downfall was spraying gloriously upwards with the wind. By the time I reached the first checkpoint at Hebden Bridge, I was leading the ladies' race. I took the opportunity to dress my bleeding knees, cross that I'd injured myself so early on and so unnecessarily.

The weather for the race was not too bad until Storm Brendan showed up. I first noticed the strengthening winds as I topped out over Dodd Fell Hill. Conditions rapidly grew wild and I raced down into Hawes, glad for the reprieve inside the support point. There I considered my options. It was about 2 p.m. so there was still some daylight to be had, and although it could have been a good move to sit the storm out where I was, the wind would be behind me, so I decided to press on.

Leaving the checkpoint, I became aware of discomfort in my right ankle. I'd bashed it the week before while clambering over the rocks at Cauldron Snout, but had thought nothing of it. I tried to ignore the pain, but soon it became unbearable and I could no longer run properly. I stopped after three kilometres, just before the ascent up Great Shunner Fell. I couldn't really see what was wrong, but the ankle was clearly swollen and it was hurting because of pressure from my shoes. I tried to tie the laces a different way and that seemed to help a bit. So I started heading up the hill and it wasn't long before the Swiss runner Simon Gfeller caught me up.

Simon was certainly able to move faster than me at that point, but he seemed happier to stick together and share the navigation. It soon became dark and as we climbed it got colder and windier still. It was also chucking it down with sleety rain, the gale so fierce we could barely hear each other. Then, as we reached the summit plateau, there was a sudden gust of wind that blew me over. My head torch fell off my head and started rolling down the hill. The light was still on, so at least I could see where it had landed, but I had to crawl over to get it because I couldn't see anything. Sorting myself out, I realised I had turned my ankle in the fall and been soaked through landing in sodden grass. Simon eventually noticed that I was no longer with him and came back to see if I was okay. We were both very cold.

Back on my feet, I tried my best to jog along but it was too painful. I could see Simon was shivering and I told him to run on without me, but he wouldn't leave. I knew I had to try my best to go as fast as I could because otherwise Simon was going to freeze. Before leaving Hawes, I had put on lots of extra layers with my huge poncho on top so, although I was not exactly warm, I was not at risk of hypothermia. We started to think about trying to find shelter to stop and put on more layers, but there was nothing until we got all the way down to Thwaite. Even there the only thing we could find to hide in was a telephone box.

We were both still a little cold, but warmed up again on the jog to Keld. I decided to stop in at the Reading Room, a much appreciated refuge just half a mile off the Pennine Way, so I could look at my ankle in the warm and dry. I knew there was a kettle there too, so I thought a brew and some food would do us good. My ankle was very swollen, but I managed to keep it raised for a bit and thanks to the Spine safety team also managed to ice it. There was not much more that could be done, but I already felt better with a hot drink and something to eat. We pressed on.

Simon and I stayed together and I was grateful for the company. At the Middleton support point, I would have spent only a few minutes to change my socks and resupply my bag, but Simon wanted to sleep for a bit and me to wait for him. I knew that wasn't the best strategy for either of us. I suspected Simon could move faster than me and I didn't need to take time to stop there, but he had been so kind, so I was happy to do as he asked. When we left Middleton, Simon was moving well and I simply couldn't keep up. It wasn't long before I had to send him on ahead. It was easier hobbling along at my own pace. How I did it I'm not sure, but I caught him up some time later at Dufton.

By then, it was snowing heavily and about to get dark again, so it seemed sensible for us to stick together over Cross Fell (893 metres), the highest point on the course. It was snowing so hard that there were no footprints to be seen from the few runners ahead. It was bitter and if we stopped for any length of time we were in danger of being frozen into the landscape. Everything was cold. My pockets were frozen shut and I couldn't open them to get a gel out. When I did, it was hard to eat with my hands numb in thick clumsy gloves that were wet and frozen. We had to keep moving and do so quickly to stay warm, but it was almost impossible while trying to navigate on slabs that were a foot under soft snow. We risked plunging into the gaps between the slabs, since we couldn't see where they were.

I knew I was critically hypothermic, but I just kept telling myself to keep going to Greg's Hut, just below Cross Fell summit on the Garrigill side, where there would be hot soup and the chance to warm up. Eventually we made it, but I had to stay in Greg's Hut for a long time to get warm again. And doing that caused my ankle to swell even more, so when I finally left the hut I was hobbling in pain again. I made Simon go on ahead so I could continue at my own pace. I didn't sleep at Alston but took a short nap in Slaggyford. I must have passed Simon and Wouter, a Dutch adventure-racing friend, as they had both gone off too hard at the beginning of the race and then taken it a bit easier to recover. Clearly, they had got their second wind and they caught me up again somewhere along Hadrian's Wall. I'm not sure how I made it to Bellingham. The daylight helped, but I was not moving well. I knew I had to stop there since I hadn't had much sleep and I didn't want to cross the Cheviots with the risk of dozing off up there. That would be dangerous. Wouter and Simon both arrived at the checkpoint about an hour before me and were sleeping when I arrived. I would have liked to join them when they left but was worried my ankle wouldn't keep up. I had to stick to my plan. After sleeping for two hours, I headed out refreshed, making good progress to Byrness and powering my way across the Cheviots, but I had to limp my way down from The Schil to Kirk Yetholm for fifth place overall.

I was glad I had made it, but I knew this would come at a cost. After ignoring the ankle injury and pushing through tendonitis, it was going to be a long road to recovery. After the Winter Spine Race, I was left crippled. I even borrowed some crutches from a client of my vet practice to help me move the short distances I needed to for daily life. How humiliating: to go from athletic prowess to a wretched, hobbling ruin of a person. It was at least two weeks before I could walk without crutches, just in time for our wedding.

I'd known I'd wanted to marry Ben within a few months of being together, but it had taken him ten years to propose. It took us a further three years to plan our wedding, probably because we were quite busy with the bunkhouse and the vet practice. When we first moved up to the Lakes, I had commuted back to my job in Surrey for a while, working nights and weekends for a long week and then coming back up north for two weeks off. While I was in Surrey, I moved back in with my parents. My dad would cook me lunch and we would chat. When I was back in the Lakes, I'd do some locum work as well, and then after about a year I found a permanent job at a practice in Carnforth. I told the owner, who was approaching retirement age, that I was interested in buying the practice, but while she was interested, in the end she decided not to sell.

So Ben and I scouted around for somewhere to start my own practice, since finding the right premises with the necessary planning permissions would be the hardest part. I'd wanted a practice in the heart of the Lake District, but having lived there for a bit we soon realised there wasn't the population density to support another business. Eventually, we found an industrial unit near Carnforth that we could readily fit out for a modern practice. This is when Ben came into his own. He has an abundance of skill in something I lack: spatial awareness. He has the ability to manipulate three-dimensional images in his brain. All that mattered to me was that I wanted a practical space. I took a piece of paper and drew a two-dimensional sketch of where I wanted the different rooms I needed: consulting rooms, X-ray, theatre, prep and so on. He took that and turned it into a snazzy three-dimensional drawing on the computer. It took five weeks to have the whole place fitted out. Ben was offered voluntary redundancy around this time from his job at Siemens and so came to work at the practice with me. This worked out well, especially when they offered him his job back eighteen months later.

On 31 January 2020, Ben and I finally got married. For the reception, we arranged a dinner and ceilidh at the beautifully located Glaramara Hotel in Borrowdale for friends and family. But while I was at least able to walk, if not run, my ankles were still sore so I couldn't dance for long periods, although this might have had more to do with trying to wear silly high heels, not something I do that much.

After the wedding I tried to get back to training but my Strava log looked pitifully thin. Between 2 and 14 February I managed only a three-kilometre run around the canal near my work. But I had only three months to get ready for my epic Wainwrights adventure, so I needed to start properly. On Friday 14 February I managed my first proper run since the Winter Spine: 14.6 kilometres over Garburn Pass without even going over the two Wainwright summits nearby: Sour Howes and Sallows.

Ben and I spent Valentine's weekend at Lyzzick Hall Hotel: my treat. I had hoped we might recce a couple of the nearby Wainwrights, but the weather was terrible and horribly unromantic. Even so, we did manage to summit Dodd. I had looked at the route Steve Birkinshaw had taken and wondered why he'd backtracked from the summit to pick up a fire road through Dodd Wood when it seemed on the map there should be a nice, direct route off the nose. So we explored the direct route and it turned out not to be nice at all but steep and littered with trip hazards like tree roots and small boulders. In those wet February conditions it was absolutely treacherous. It was also unbearably slow. I would be going the same way Steve had.

On the Sunday I managed to convince Ben to do a 'long run' (still too short for me) and we bagged Sale Fell, Ling Fell, Kirk Fell, Broom Fell, Lord's Seat and Barf. I was nowhere near running my best, but at least I felt able to run, even if it was slow and unsustainable. Things could only get better as I regained fitness and the days got longer. And it was great to be back out there.

The last couple of weeks of February were still quite cold and windy. I had tried to get some more recces in but had abandoned some overambitious efforts. 'Eyes bigger than legs', as a wise runner once said. I find it a useful phrase to describe so many of my runs that I set out on only to discover I've bitten off more than I can chew. Most of the time I would head out on my own to recce sections that took my fancy. Some days I would rope in a willing accomplice.

As my training picked up momentum, Ben and I, like the rest of the world, were becoming aware of Covid-19 and the impact it was having in China. In February it had reached Italy and I became increasingly alarmed as I watched news reports showing how Italian hospitals were being overrun and deaths were escalating. Yet in Britain we did nothing. It wasn't until 16 March that the government took the first steps to tackling the situation by stopping non-essential travel. I was lucky I hadn't planned to go anywhere and continued my work as a vet, running when I could. Then suddenly the pandemic took over, affecting every nation and every person and changing our lives forever.

FIVE

BREAKING THE LAW?

On 23 March, just as my training was hitting its stride, the country went into lockdown. I think a lot of us were confused about the new rules and laws, and it took some adjusting to cope with all our freedoms suddenly being taken away by Covid-19. I was so thankful that here in the UK at least we were allowed to exercise and escape outdoors. Living in Great Langdale, I was a lot luckier than most: I had the fells on my doorstep.

The problems came in all the confusion around what was legal and what was socially acceptable. Understandably, farmers in my valley were concerned about catching Covid-19 from tourists breaking the law. One day during the lockdown I went for a run, leaving from my home and heading up The Band, the long ridge that extends to the top of Bow Fell. This took me on to a bridleway that goes through the farm at the end of our road.

'What do you think you're doing?' the farmer yelled at me.

'I'm your neighbour and I'm using this public bridleway to access the fells.' I decided just to keep running. After all, we were more likely to give each other the virus if we stood shouting at each other. As I ran, I contemplated what I was doing: taking my one permitted exercise of the day. I hadn't driven anywhere. I was only a mile from my house. So, yes, what I was doing was legal. But was it socially acceptable?

I considered how the farmer might be feeling: worried, perhaps scared she could get Covid-19 – it would be a serious problem for the animals if she got sick. She has a diabetic son; he's in the vulnerable group of people who have a higher than average risk of death. But if she was acting out of genuine fear, it was also true that even at the best of times she wasn't happy about having a bridleway through the farm. And this definitely wasn't the best of times.

I gave myself a reality check. I definitely didn't have Covid-19. During this period, while there was some debate about whether vets were key workers, I was going to work every day. Owning the practice meant I was able to make quick decisions about how best to handle the situation. I was in the fortunate position of working on my own, thanks to some lucky timing. The vet who had been working for me for a year had handed in her notice just as Covid-19 was kicking off, when cases were rising dramatically in Italy. My student veterinary nurse was on maternity leave and I had been using a locum to cover her shifts. So I went to work on my own, meaning I felt completely safe. I didn't let another person in the practice for three weeks. When I arrived, I locked the front door and put a notice up asking clients to phone when they arrived. I had cats placed in a basket on the doorstep and dogs tied to the fence post. This way I could collect the animal while maintaining more than two metres' distance from people. As a vet I was already well equipped to deal with the situation. I owned all the necessary personal protective equipment because I wear it on a daily basis. I wore a mask to protect both others and myself and I was already using medical-grade hand sanitiser anyway.

Normally, when a vet physically examines an animal, it's useful to have either the owner or a nurse restrain them. So I had to get inventive when taking temperatures and placing intravenous catheters. It wasn't the first time I had needed to do this. When I first graduated, things were different from the way they are now. The weekends were crazy busy and we had no nurse on call, so I often had to look after inpatients all on my own.

Apart from seeing animals that required emergency treatment, I also wanted to stay on top of preventative healthcare. You might assume that flea treatment, tick control, worming and vaccination isn't urgent, but if you let these lapse then you see more sick animals. Cats particularly can become anaemic from a flea infestation and young puppies are at high risk of dying from roundworm infection. So I found a big plastic, waterproof box with a lid and put in all the medications, flea treatments and so forth that needed dispensing. When clients were on their way to collect these, I popped the box outside with a bottle of hand sanitiser on top. I put an invoice in the prescription bag with the drugs; clients could pay online or on the phone. Those I saw were so grateful I could still help their pets. Professionally speaking, I have never been happier.

During the first lockdown, the practice saw a dramatic drop in turnover. I was down to twenty-five per cent of what I would normally bring in. As a consequence, I had to work more hours myself. I couldn't afford to pay anyone else to do it. Plus, paying for help might have been more trouble than it was worth, with the laws and guidelines changing, it sometimes felt, on a daily basis. It would be hard to keep employees safe and keep up with all the health and safety documentation. I figured I could save myself time just working on my own. That meant I had to cover all the out-of-hours work myself as well as being at work every day we were open. I also had to do all the cleaning in the practice and all the administration, like answering the phone and emails. I also had to order stock, check it in and put it away, doing all the boring tasks like checking fridge and freezer temperatures.

One morning I arrived to discover one of my pharmacy fridges had decided to turn itself into an oven. When I went to check its temperature it was 43° Celsius. The vaccines inside were all cooked. I had no choice but to throw away £4,000 worth of stock. With setbacks like that, the financial side of things was getting a bit thin. On top of that, clients were starting to want to cancel their pet-health plans. Many were self-employed, hair-dressers for example, and they had to start cutting down where they could. People didn't understand that the payments were to cover my costs of supplying products up front. I didn't even make money from these plans; they only just covered the costs of vaccinations and treatments supplied. So pressure was building on me. I still had to find maternity pay, settle drugs invoices, meet repayments on loans for equipment and keep finding the rent and all the other regular expenses. And I needed a new fridge. At least the weather was dry and sunny. When it all got a bit much, I just put on my running shoes and forwarded the phones to my mobile. Then I'd be gone to the fells, clearing my head and easing my woes.

If I was isolated at work, then it wasn't so different at home, since Ben was working there alone. We had been having most of our food delivered anyway, a box of fresh ingredients and recipes for four. We'd cook for dinner and keep the leftovers for lunch next day. The only things I needed to buy in a supermarket were fresh fruit and milk. I felt so fortunate living in the Lake District. The shops in Ambleside were more or less empty, since in reality not that many people live there. You might see one or two people, but everyone sanitised their hands on the way in and kept their distance. That wasn't the case in Kendal; it seemed people living in urban areas were much less capable of social distancing and most couldn't grasp the concept of one-way systems. So I avoided bigger towns.

Pausing on the bridleway at Stool End Farm, I knew it was highly unlikely that I would get the virus and, even if I did, I really wasn't going to pass it on to the farmer or her family by running on the track through their farm. Yet I wanted to be considerate of their feelings and understood that the fear of catching Covid-19 could cause them unnecessary stress. So I decided to take alternative routes for a few weeks until the whole thing calmed down. I had other places I could run.

I had to keep my runs to within a tight distance of the practice so I could get back to work quickly in the event of an emergency. So it was and is a privilege that I live and work in such beautiful places. From work, I can run up on to Hutton Roof and from its trig point you can see out to Morecambe Bay, the beautiful Lake District mountains and the grassy mounds in the Howgills and the Yorkshire Dales. I can run on the peaceful track through Leighton Moss RSPB with the tall reeds and gentle twitter of birds. I can run through the woods on Cringlebarrow and into the meadows at Gait Barrows Nature Reserve. I can run up the hill out the back of Yealand and admire the view down to Leighton Hall and over the coast. This really is an area of outstanding natural beauty. What was I worrying about? Cash flow? On the fells it seemed so insignificant. As poor as one can be, nature is priceless and the mountains are there to be run over.

After adjusting to the initial shock of the new laws, we started to accept that

Covid-19 was not going away, and rather than being a three-week inconvenience it was starting to look like a year-long saga. The 23 March lockdown was extended for a further three weeks. I became concerned about how long I could keep the practice running. The financial aid from the local council was a lifeline: the £10,000 business grant would keep me afloat until 'things got back to normal', a phrase we would all be using for years to come.

A lot of businesses were panicking. All of the other local vet practices had needed to furlough most of their staff and shut their branch practices. It was a risky but opportune moment for me to take on a new vet. Everyone else was scaling down, but I felt that the veterinary industry would have an inevitable rebound to catch up on all the missed work, a bit like the NHS. I found a very good locum looking for work to cover her mortgage payments. Good vets are hard to find so I seized the opportunity and, although I thought things might be tight for me financially, I was happy to give her two days a week and have two days off for my running, a much-needed break for me.

Those two days a week were blissful. The weather was incredible and I had a lot of recces to do for my Wainwrights challenge, although it was still uncertain what the rules were in relation to exercising outdoors. There was definitely a restriction in that you were not allowed to exercise more than once a day, but there was not a firm limit on how long that period of exercise could be. In London, where outdoor space was limited and easily crowded, it seemed sensible to restrict exercise to an hour, although I think this was advice and not mandatory. It did seem rather absurd to have any restriction on those in rural areas like myself, where I could have run for days on end and not seen another soul.

Unfortunately, there were many people with a lot of time on their hands and nothing better to do than moan on social media about other people who they thought were breaking the rules. It all got so ridiculous. I decided to go 'dark' on Strava. There was absolutely no need to show off about all the amazing running I could do from my doorstep while some poor folk were stuck in a one-bedroom flat in central London, and I didn't need to be the victim of some bored person who wanted to have a go.

Ben got used to me leaving the house on my days off with a large rucksack packed full of food and 'seven essentials'. This was a trick I had learnt at school when we did hikes to qualify for the Duke of Edinburgh Award, packing seven essential items: compass, map, gloves, hat, whistle, head torch and waterproofs. He even stopped asking how long I was going to be, because I usually replied that I had no idea. The Wainwrights that I had left to recce were all on the Western Fells. And because it was unclear at that time whether we were allowed to drive to exercise, and if so how far, I only allowed myself to run from my doorstep at home or from the practice. That removed any temptation to drive somewhere further afield to do a recce. It seemed important to play by the rules. (Unless of course I needed my eyesight testing, in which case Barnard Castle seemed a reasonable choice.)

Setting off from home, I would choose some fells I hadn't been to before. For example, one day I decided to bag Seatallan and Middle Fell. Seatallan is about sixteen kilometres from my door as the crow flies. Unfortunately there were a few mountains in the way, so I had to negotiate them en route to the start of my recce. I headed out from Langdale along the Cumbrian Way, taking the left fork to head up to Angle Tarn. This took about an hour. Then I trotted on past the Esk Hause shelter to Sprinkling Tarn. I then made my way down to Wasdale Head and continued west along Wast Water. From the car park at Overbeck Bridge I turned right, heading up the footpath that follows the beck, thereby skirting Yewbarrow. As I ascended, I looked towards Yewbarrow for possible lines of descent, as I would most likely come from there to climb Seatallan. It all looked quite steep and rocky, but I spotted a gully that looked a bit easier and grassier. I decided to check out that line next time I was over this way. Then I headed up to where this descent line would lead me on to a plateau: Gosforth Crag Moss.

This pathless terrain looked like it might be tricky to cross on the map and proved to be worth exploring. It was the end of April, so it was a bit chilly and the ground was still very boggy. I slowed down, sharply negotiating the various wet, grassy tussocks and all the jagged rocks strewn in between. Eventually, after some hard work, I reached Blackbeck Knotts and still had to negotiate a rather steep rock descent around its crag. I looked towards Seatallan and Middle Fell and contemplated whether it was worth switching the order and heading to Middle Fell first because it's lower. Instead, I stuck with the plan and tackled the long climb using Rowantree

Gill as a navigational handrail, ascending from 340 metres to the summit at 692 metres.

That last section was tiring. I wouldn't be looking forward to that bit when I reached it on the Wainwrights Round. In the coming months these fells were going to be even harder to cross as they became smothered in bracken. I checked the time and blinked. It had taken me nearly four hours just to get to this one summit. So I hurried along to bag Middle Fell, happily descending a good grassy footpath, and made the relatively short ascent (110 metres) to the summit (582 metres). I then took a moment to admire the view. Although it was a bit claggy, I could see Wast Water and the ridgeline behind with two more Wainwrights: Whin Rigg and Illgill Head. They would have to be tackled another day. I was always sad to turn for home on these explorations, even if my legs were tired and I wanted to rest. It was disappointing to have to retrace my steps instead of carrying on my adventure. If I hadn't had work to do I'd have happily carried on through the night and beyond.

I continued doing recces in this fashion throughout the glorious months of April and May, averaging 100 kilometres per week and 6,000 metres of height gain. I never had a training plan but these recces were naturally conditioning my body to the fells day after day. From Monday to Thursday, while I was working, I generally rested, with a short run near the practice on Wednesdays. Then I had big days out on Friday, Saturday and Sunday. I felt great and was clearly getting stronger. I never focused on running quickly while I was doing the recces. I was going at a pace where I could navigate and explore the route options.

From 14 May, the rules on exercise were relaxed a little, allowing people greater access to local outdoor physical activity. The public were now allowed to go outside for unlimited exercise, alone or with their household, or with one other person while adhering to social distancing rules. This was amazing. I could run with a friend again. On 22 May I met up with my La Sportiva teammate Jacob Snochowski in Patterdale to recce the Helvellyn leg. It was clear and sunny but a bit chilly with a strong wind: a lovely day to be out, and we covered twenty kilometres in two and a half hours with a height gain of 2,500 metres.

It was incredible to have someone else alongside me to share the fell eye candy. Jacob is a strong runner and I knew this route quite well, so we made quick progress up Birks, on to St Sunday Crag and then to Seat Sandal. This was a section of Steve Birkinshaw's route that I had wanted to change, taking Seat Sandal on this leg instead of approaching it from Fairfield. It seemed a good choice as this approach felt pretty easy and the descent down to Grisedale Tarn was grassy and fun. Heading up to Dollywaggon Pike, we could tell the wind was picking up, but we were still sheltered as we climbed. As we reached the summit, however, it was ferocious. Where had that come from? Jacob pulled away as we headed to Helvellyn and I was then blown off my feet a couple of times. In the distance I could see Jacob was also finding it hard to stay on his feet.

Heading out to Catstye Cam, I decided, would be too dangerous. We would have to negotiate Swirral Edge, which with its exposed drop-offs can be lethal. There was still some snow and ice on the ground that would also make it slippery. I might easily be caught by a gust and plummet to my death. As I was thinking this, I got caught by a massive gust and started accelerating towards Jacob; he was likewise picked up by the gust and blown over. I was skidding completely out of control towards the cliff edge just off Helvellyn's summit and had to throw myself to the ground to stop. *Ouch,* I thought. *That hurt … although not nearly as much as going off the side.* Having given up on Catstye Cam, we elected to head straight down to Glenridding, the easiest and safest route over Lower Man, and then down the bridleway that joins the mining track. We had a huge tailwind and so were down in no time. We'd missed not only Catstye Cam but the summit of Birkhouse Moor as well, but it was worth it to stay safe.

The end of May approached and I was getting impatient for the rules to ease further. I felt fit and ready to take on the Wainwrights. We'd had six weeks of lovely sunny weather, the ground was dry and the bracken was only just starting to shoot up: conditions were perfect. But how long would they last? *Come on, Boris,* I thought, *give us our freedom.* Finally, at the end of that week, the government announced that from 1 June we were allowed to do unlimited exercise and we could meet in groups of up to six. I interpreted this as Boris's personal blessing to me: 'Go and do the Wainwrights.'

On Friday 29 May 2020, I completed a final recce of Harter Fell and

Green Crag (fourteen kilometres and 670 metres of height gain), a recce I had had to abandon in the winter because of all the snow. Later that afternoon, I joined Tom Gibbs and my husband Ben on a run up the Old Man, Swirl How and Wetherlam. The cogs were already turning and I asked Tom about his availability for support the following week. I decided there and then I would go for it on Tuesday 2 June. I got home and started on the spreadsheet, organising supporters for the first attempt, starting at 3 a.m. from Keswick Moot Hall with Kim Collison.

To complete the Wainwrights as quickly as possible requires a good support team. I wouldn't say that any one person is key to a successful round; what is needed is a large number of competent fell runners and a capable and reliable road support team. My first and second attempts on the Wainwrights were organised with minimal backing. John Knapp was doing a lot of the road support points with his car and Ben with his. We didn't have a camper van then. The third and fourth attempts were much better organised, with camper vans at most of the support points. This meant we could look after the larger support team as well.

A road support team really needs to know their job: what they're doing, where they're going, where they can park, from which direction they're expecting runners to arrive. They need to know which support runners are on the current leg and the next one, and they need to be organised and efficient. There isn't a lot of time when I come flying in and plan to leave again in less than five minutes, sometimes not stopping at all. So either Ben or my friend Debs needed to make sure the pacers had my spare kit, the trackers, the food for the leg, the first-aid kit and the maps. If I was running ahead or behind schedule, someone had to be in charge of relaying this information to the team. By the fourth attempt, everyone seemed just to know exactly what they were doing, like a well-oiled machine.

I first met Debs White on the Dragon's Back Race in 2019. She was on the support team and had gone to fetch my drop bag at the end of the race. She returned some forty minutes later, explaining that she had accidentally managed to lock herself in the back of the truck that all the bags were in and she'd had to use her mobile to call for someone to let her out! Despite this mishap, as it turned out Debs would become my number-one road support for future records including the Pennine Way and the Wainwrights Round. In return, I would become the personal physician for her three fabulous border collies.

I had to work extra hard with the logistics because I was mindful of all the Covid-19 rules; I was determined to minimise any risk to my support team. I limited it to one person on the hill with me and just one vehicle. I used only Lakeland supporters and made sure the legs they were doing were local to them. I was lucky most people were available and flexible because everyone was either working from home or furloughed. I planned only to sleep at my own house forty-eight hours into the round and to take power naps on the fell after that.

Everyone was keen to be involved because quite frankly there was nothing else to do: no races, no pubs, no cafes. I took every precaution I could think of to stay within the rules. Yet I knew that doing the round at that time would be controversial and so I asked my support team to keep it to themselves. I hired a tracker from Open Tracking and shared the link with my support team only. I wanted to keep it between ourselves, and was trying to avoid any media attention.

At some point, Martin Stone got in touch. Martin was well known on the fell-running scene, winner of the first Dragon's Back along with Helen Diamantides and now managing director of the time-keeping entry system we all use. Martin had caught wind of what I wanted to do and advised me that the round would not be ratified because they weren't ratifying Bob Graham rounds at that time. That sounded good to me. I didn't want it ratified anyway. I wasn't chasing a record or doing it for fame and fortune. I wanted to do the journey as one complete round as a personal challenge, just to see if I could do it in less than six days. Then I started to realise this was bugging other people.

'What if you break the record?' they asked. I wasn't bothered about 'the record'. That wasn't important to me. Consequently, I set off perfectly happy in the knowledge that if I did beat Paul Tierney's time it would not be officially acknowledged. And I was absolutely fine with that. After all, Steve and Paul would both be supporting me on a leg. Who else would need to know that I'd even done the round?

SIX
READY, STEADY, STOP!

Finally, the kit boxes that had been clogging up our garage for six weeks had all been packed. My spreadsheet was complete. On the first night in June 2020 I was madly marking my route on OS maps, having just realised I needed to give these to my support team so they knew where we were going. I loaded John Knapp's car with what I needed for the first two days and hoped the rest would take care of itself. I'd be back home in forty-eight hours for some kip and Ben would come out with the rest of the stuff over the weekend.

Tuesday 2 June. 2 a.m. My alarm went off. I stuffed some pastries in my mouth while pulling on my running clothes. I slurped some tea and threw myself and my packed running vest into the car. It was 2.20 a.m. and dark, wet and windy. Driving to Keswick, excited about the adventure I was about to begin, I was also a little disappointed that the weather was not quite how I imagined. Where was that clear starry night and bright, full moon? I parked on Brundholme Road and grabbed my stuff. Meanwhile, James Thurlow was fretting that it was almost 3 a.m. and my tracker was not at Moot Hall. James owns the company Open Tracking, providing tracking devices for all the dot watchers online to follow runners. I, on the other hand, was feeling quite relaxed as I jogged over to Moot Hall, where

I arrived at 2.59 a.m. Perfect timing. I could see Kim Collison's head torch shining through the fine mist. I met Kim through adventure racing, but he is better known as a fell runner and holder of the esteemed Lakeland 24-hour record. I greeted him by handing over my packed running vest to carry as well as his own.

As it turned out, handicapping Kim Collison with two running packs meant he ran at exactly the right pace for me, unencumbered as I was with any extra weight. Although wet, conditions were quite warm and it wasn't long before I got rid of my waterproof: something else for Kim to carry. Reaching Latrigg in good time, we continued across Brundholme Bridge, which had just been repaired, and made our way effortlessly along the roads towards High Rigg. Somehow we then managed to go slightly off route through some undergrowth as we missed a turning on to a footpath. It was a minor error and, despite the slightly less than perfect navigation, covering ground in such wonderfully dry conditions meant I was easily gaining time on my schedule. Climbing Bleaberry Fell, I told Kim it felt like it was going to be a hot day: it wasn't even 5 a.m. but the temperature was already over 20° Celsius. It did indeed grow hotter and hotter, but I loved it. Kim was less comfortable in 27° sunshine, but being so strong didn't need to push to keep up with me. He would often sprint on ahead to get photos of me at the summits.

The only problem was getting enough water. By the time we crossed Armboth Fell we had run out and had to continue for an hour or so until the larger stream crossing of Blea Tarn Gill to fill up because all the smaller streams had dried up. On the plus side, because it was so dry, the river crossing at Rosthwaite was relatively easy and, other than soaking my dry socks in water, painless. Heading up to Castle Crag, we managed to get the line a little wrong (a mistake I managed to repeat on the fourth attempt). Yet, despite this, it seemed Kim was gathering momentum as we approached the end of his leg and I sprinted into Borrowdale almost twenty minutes up on my schedule. A quick change of socks and I was off with Jeff Powell Davies, heading up to Bessyboot, then Glaramara and within two hours reaching Allen Crag.

Neil Talbott, secretary of the Fell Runners Association, met us there; he was concerned that I was going too fast, but I felt good. I was drinking plenty now we had refilled and he was adding two Zero electrolyte tabs to every litre of water. I seemed to be consuming a colossal amount of food as well, but I thought this was much better than eating too little.

I couldn't believe how quickly we negotiated the tricky terrain to Seathwaite Tarn down and then back up to Base Brown, and before I knew it we were on Hay Stacks. It was so much easier following Neil than it had been navigating on my own and carrying all my own provisions. The ground was so easy when it was this dry; you could skip across rocky steps untroubled by thoughts of slipping and tumbling. The downside was the scorching temperature; we would be completely exposed to the sun's powerful rays the whole way along this beautiful Buttermere ridge. Neil had picked up a whopping six litres of water at Black Beck (our last water stop until Loweswater). I had thought it was a ludicrously large amount, but apparently I had drunk it all by the end of the leg!

At Loweswater I met my third-leg man, Mike Robinson. Mike completed this leg with me three times and would have made it four if I'd actually made it that far on all my attempts, since on my third and fourth tries, which I started at Langdale, this leg became number twenty. On all three occasions it was sunny and Mike knew exactly where he was going: no map required. Mike's an extremely handy fell runner with the most impressive head of long blond hair like a lion's mane.

At Ennerdale, as night began to fall, I headed up Grike with my good friend Tom Gibbs. I've been privileged to pair up with Tom for the Marmot Dark Mountains race. In fact, we've won the elite pairs race three times, no thanks to me. The third time I wouldn't consider a true victory because we won by default. I had not been nearly as fit as I should have been and found it impossible to keep up with Tom for most of the night. He had to tow me at one point in the Forest of Bowland by clipping a rope to his rucksack that attached to my waistbelt. We called that climb 'Jelly Mountain' because it had been lashing down all night and the grassy tussocks were so sodden they literally felt like walking on wobbly jelly. The only useful thing I did all race was get a second wind for the final hour, when we managed to sprint past Steve Birkinshaw's team for what I thought was third place, only to get promoted when the teams ahead of us were disqualified, including Neil

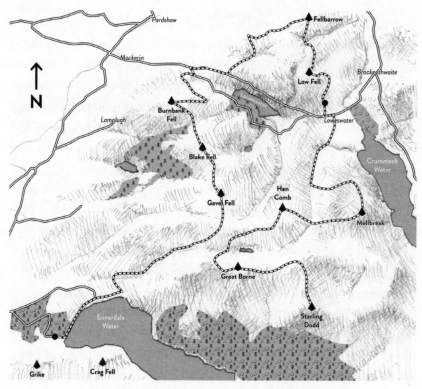

Leg 3 of attempts 1 and 2 (Keswick start) and leg 20 of attempts 3 and 4 (Langdale start).

Talbott's team in second. I felt for them because they had completed the course a country mile ahead of us.

This stretch of the Wainwrights began well but it was spitting by the time we hit Haycock. That deteriorated in short order to a torrential downpour and the wind started to pick up too. It was slippery underfoot, wet and wild; Tom and I could barely hear each other. Navigation became hard and we were concerned we wouldn't find a trod up the side of Yewbarrow from Red Pike, familiar from the Bob Graham Round, so we made the mistake of following the footpath directly up the nose, quite a hard, steep scramble in the rain. The wet, bracken-infested slog up Seatallan was depressingly slow going and at the summit we were greeted by a howling wind. At least as we headed off Middle Fell we had a tailwind – a very strong tailwind that blew us all the way to Buckbarrow and down to Nether Wasdale, where we landed at least two hours ahead of schedule.

We were both glad to be off the fell and climbing into James's camper van. It had been a challenging night. I started to get changed, ready for the next leg, while simultaneously eating a hot meal. James, however, had something to tell me.

'Sabs, Andy Slattery has told us that what we are doing is illegal.' He paused. Andy Slattery was the assistant chief constable of Cumbria and a local fell runner. 'But it's okay, we are all happy to continue if that's what you want to do.'

Ouch. Just like that, a completely unexpected blow had thrown me. It wasn't the catastrophic injury I'd feared; it wasn't a crazy insane hurricane that had come out of nowhere or a major navigational booboo. Problems like those, although random and often uncontrollable, had at least crossed my mind, or even happened to me before. This came completely out of the blue.

I didn't have to think long and hard about what came next. If Andy Slattery had managed to get this message to me all the way in Nether Wasdale, then I had to stop. I didn't believe that running like this could be illegal; I had spent so long looking into all the Covid-19 rules. But I also saw that my team had made various attempts to clarify this with Andy and to explore possible exceptions to the rules. There was, for example, an exception made for elite runners, who did not have to 'stay at home'. Even so, I thought it best to stop, go home and speak to Andy to try and understand the situation.

We sent a message to the team on our WhatsApp group to let everyone know what was happening and we parted feeling low and unfulfilled. I got home and had a bath. I didn't feel that tired, given that I had been running continuously for over twenty-four hours and at a good pace. This made the situation all the harder to swallow. My Wainwrights attempt, something I had been building towards for six years, had been going so fabulously to plan and then the rug had been pulled out from under my feet. I was crosser with myself than with Andy, who was just doing his job. I should have waited out the Covid-19 thing a bit longer. When I called Andy, he said that the stay-at-home law was still in place and explained what it actually meant. I had interpreted it to mean that you weren't allowed to stay the night anywhere other than your house. This made sense to me. We shouldn't be in hotels or friends' houses because this could increase the spread of the virus. But I hadn't appreciated that despite the relaxation of the rules, we were still legally obliged to go home every night, and that while Boris had said we could do 'unlimited exercise', he didn't actually mean it.

It was confusing. There was no curfew set. To be honest, none of it made any sense at all: at least, not to me. What did it matter if I spent all night running on the hills? That wouldn't increase the risk of spreading Covid-19. Andy agreed and said he would speak to the legal department to get clarification. It was important for me to find out, because if it wasn't illegal I did want to get back out there and try again. Andy got back to me the next day and explained that others had been challenging the law. Apart from running, anglers had been asking why overnight fishing had been deemed illegal. This too made no sense. One fisherman in a tent by the side of a lake all night is no greater risk than during the day. However, despite it not making sense, Andy was clear: while the stay-at-home law was in place, all of us had to return to our dwelling once in every twenty-four-hour period. At least I knew now where I stood. Andy promised to give me a heads-up when he knew the date the law would change, and I prepared to wait.

I could understand Andy's perspective. He had been involved with Paul Tierney's record-breaking round in 2019, which was hardly low-key. At times there were various runners out on the hill, a camera crew following him, multiple camper vans and cars with the support crew, masseurs and lots of bystanders at key points. So I understood if Andy thought my attempt would be the same, and I'm sure he imagined the worst with crowds gathering and contracting the virus; he quite rightly thought it would be best to put an end to it before I had gone too far and was later stopped by someone else. I knew it would have caused him pain, but better at that point than after I had invested myself in many more miles.

The days ticked by and I grew increasingly frustrated scanning for news about the lifting of the stay at home order. And then finally I got the heads-up from Andy Slattery: 4 July. Independence Day. How appropriate. I wasted no time in summoning the troops, sending a quick Facebook message to see who might be free for about a week from around Friday 3 July. Having talked to Andy about the rules, it was clear that without a curfew, as long as I spent some of the day at home, there was no reason I couldn't start on 3 July. Everyone was still excited by the project, especially as the first attempt had come to such a premature end. I rewrote the schedule and filled in pacers for a 3 a.m. start on 3 July. But as we approached the start date, the weather was predicted to turn. Those glorious dry ground conditions were turning soggy and the endless sunny days had finally come to an end.

Then on 28 June I got a message from Neil Talbott, the secretary of the FRA who had supported me on leg two of the first attempt. While not a meteorologist, Neil is a hugely experienced fell runner and lives close by in Chapel Stile.

'I don't want to be pessimistic, but have you seen the latest forecast for next weekend?'

The Friday and Saturday looked like constant rain. It wouldn't be record-breaking conditions, I told Neil, but I could still do it in a reasonable time.

'I'm sure you can,' he replied, 'but keep an eye on it. Constant very strong wind is also likely.'

I agreed the wind looked bad and considered moving the start date back a day. That was all I thought I could manage. But on Wednesday 1 July things didn't look that much better. The Friday deluge was still happening but the winds were predicted to be less strong. Saturday seemed moderately wet and windy, while Sunday was drier but windier. The forecast on the Monday onwards seemed better. I messaged Neil again for advice.

'I don't want to mess up the whole schedule,' I told Neil. 'I thought I would keep my eye on the weather and wait for that deluge of rain to pass and then start on the schedule at whatever day or time seems to be better weather.' At that moment it seemed I could start from Langdale on Sunday at 5 a.m. and continue on the schedule, tacking Langdale to Keswick on at the end. 'What do you think?' I asked him.

'Okay, honest opinions. Friday is a complete no-go. Saturday is still wet and windy and Sunday is really windy. The wind will continue unabated until at least Monday evening, and Tuesday is looking like another very wet day. Obviously the forecasts can change, but if they don't, then personally I would not be starting before the wind and rain ease off on Tuesday night (and even then it is likely to be far from perfect, though much better). I obviously appreciate that you have other constraints, such as work, and that it's potentially problematic to move the schedule around. But on the latter, I think more or less everyone would rather have their plans change than spend a miserable few hours on the hill for an attempt which realistically is going to end at best in a mediocre (by your standards) completion time. I think you're capable of doing this in max seven days and possibly breaking Paul's record, but not in these conditions.'

Neil continued checking the forecast and on Thursday it was clear that the winds would stay strong through Monday before dropping markedly that evening. Then, apart from one wet day on the following Wednesday, it looked pretty decent. 'If it were me,' Neil messaged me, 'I would bin Sunday now and would be planning to start on either Monday evening/Tuesday morning (once the wind has dropped) or – ideally – Thursday morning.'

I was still in a quandary. The further ahead we looked, the less certain the weather would be. What looked like low winds, sun and decent weather in a week's time could easily turn to be similar to what we were facing now. I explained to Neil that I didn't have the luxury of time.

'I cannot sort more days off work. Ben is already fed up with me as well. So it's either Sunday or no-go and I would really like to do this. However, I now have the wrong support on the first leg out of Langdale; they may struggle with nav[igating] and speed. I feel cheeky asking, but are you able to get me off to a good start?'

Neil understood I was desperate to get moving, but put it succinctly: 'Sunday is not a day to be on the fells. Monday is still windy but sufficiently better than Sunday that it might be tolerable (if still somewhat debilitating). But if you're determined to start on Sunday morning then, yes, I can do the leg from Langdale. Alternatively, I could do Monday or Tuesday if I work Sunday.'

I knew he was right. I rearranged work so I could start on the Monday and shifted the start line to Keswick to get the three long legs done in better weather.

That made sense to Neil but he added a warning: 'It's difficult because that means Monday will be a very tough day into a strong westerly wind. On the other hand, next week is unpredictable, so if you start in Langdale then Monday will be easier, but then the bad weather on (roughly) Wednesday could come on a long/high leg.' He had checked out the Mountain Weather Information Service forecast, which was promising wind speeds up to sixty-fives miles per hour for the Sunday morning with severe wind chill. 'Based on all forecasts,' he concluded, 'I would expect Monday to be more like twenty-five to thirty-five miles per hour, gusting forty-five miles per hour.'

So it was decided. The second attempt would start on Monday 6 July at 3 a.m. at Keswick Moot Hall.

In my enforced delay, I had enjoyed spending time poring over Steve's route using my most treasured gift from Harvey Maps: a giant A1 map of the Wainwrights. In planning the round, I had thoroughly disassembled the route like a giant puzzle and put it back together many times, changing the order of summits or drastically altering entire sections and then re-looping it. Somehow, each time I did this I would once again find myself with an almost identical route.

After I had been through this process and gone out to recce sections, I would sometimes come back with a new idea. This would often result from having gone through what I called a 'shitfest'. For example, the ascent to Grisedale Pike involves clambering over a load of fallen trees and then mashing through knee-high heather up a very steep slope. I came back from that recce looking for some way to avoid this particular shitfest. Another example was the boggy, bracken-infested, tussock slog from Slight Side to Scafell. Oh, how I looked for a way round it. Of course there were ways to avoid this sort of thing, but doing so often made the route longer, or involved more ascent and descent. It was always a compromise.

Once, after recceing the descent off Lingmoor into Langdale, I considered not dropping into Langdale at all and instead approaching Lingmoor from Pike o' Blisco, where there would be less height loss and gain. However,

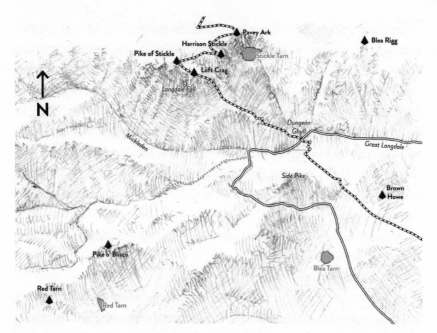

The route from Brown How dropping all the way into Langdale before ascending to Loft Crag. I considered an alternative route from Loft Crag to Pike o' Blisco that loses much less height.

trying to put this back into the loop meant the approach to Loughrigg would come directly from Black Fell. That created a problem. Ideally, you want to head due north to hit Skelwith Bridge, but there isn't a right of way. In fact, the whole of Black Fell is sealed on the OS map with an orange boundary line, demarcating open-access land on the fell from private farmland or private woods between the boundary and the public highway. This presented me with a conundrum.

We are so very lucky in the Lake District to be blessed with lots of open-access land. It's what makes Lakeland a fell-running paradise. I feel privileged to be able to exercise these rights of access over such wonderfully wild places. I enjoy the freedom of being able to leave the beaten track of the public footpaths and bridleways. So I feel a need to protect this right, because I would be saddened to have it taken away. I feel a duty to respect these boundaries and adhere to the Countryside Code. I remember being taught these rules at primary school in the 1980s when we were being educated about national parks.

The Countryside Code has its roots in the work of a variety of organisations from the 1930s onwards, with the most widely accepted version being published in 1981. It's familiar stuff: being respectful; guarding against fire risk; keeping pets under control; leaving gates as you find them. It used to be promoted on television in government commercials, especially in the 1970s. That's no longer the case. The government now spends almost nothing on promoting it. But in 2004 the Countryside Code was revised to reflect the introduction of new access legislation, the Countryside and Rights of Way Act 2000, which gave open access to upland and uncultivated land in England and Wales. (In Scotland the access situation is very different and much better.)

I developed a greater understanding of how to be respectful using open-access land when I started racing in mountain marathons. These marathons often involve two days on the fells, requiring competitors to camp overnight and navigate to checkpoints, often in a pair for safety. They are always on open-access land and race rules prescribe that you can be disqualified or penalised for crossing non-open-access land not on a public footpath or bridleway. These rules are important to follow because if hundreds of fell runners trample over private farmland it upsets the owners, racers get a bad name and as a consequence we won't be allowed to race.

I have the same philosophy when I'm out running on my own. I make sure that I'm acting responsibly. I use a map that highlights the location of the open-access boundary. Often there's a physical boundary too, like a drystone wall or a fence, but not always. Of course, it's still possible to make a mistake and I have to admit that on occasion I have made some grave navigational error and ended up off-piste on non-access land. Even so, I try my best to avoid this. And in a race it's completely unacceptable to cut a corner across non-access land to gain advantage. When I was recceing the Wainwrights I was very mindful of this. For me, cutting across private land to take a shortcut would be cheating, and indeed there are places where the route could be shortened immensely by doing so.

I only mention these things as they were important to me. I wanted to do the Wainwrights in a way that was acceptable to me. It wasn't to satisfy anyone else, but if my self-imposed rules were more stringent and forced me to increase the length of my route, then so be it. I knew I wouldn't be happy doing it any other way. I also hoped I could improve the route for others and set a good example: a small contribution, but one that meant we fell runners would not get a bad reputation and would protect all our rights that were long fought for.

Some PhD students from the University of Manchester decided to do a thesis on whether mapping technology could improve the Wainwrights route, using algorithms to make route choices: paths versus pathless terrain, elevation changes and distances. They believed they could make the route more efficient by about two per cent. When I analysed their route, I found that they had ignored the open-access boundaries; their route went where it pleased and took some ridiculously steep, rough descents that would trash a fell runner's knees, feet and quads. I concluded that the algorithm was a useful guide but ultimately couldn't beat experience.

When I set off on my recces it was helpful to have the GPX trace of Steve Birkinshaw's route on my watch. As Paul had followed Steve's route more or less exactly, with only small refinements, I had downloaded Paul's freely available trace from Strava as well. It was interesting to look back on the five years between the two attempts and see just how much technology has changed. When Steve set off, the whole concept of 'dot watching' was just beginning. By the time Paul did his round in 2019, it was all the rage. I knew that if I made my 'dot' publicly visible, then a great number of people would be watching my progress and following my route. And I wanted my route to be as 'clean' as possible. I wanted to make sure that if someone down-loaded my Strava track and set off with it on their watch, it would not lead them astray across private farmland. I didn't want people being stopped by an angry farmer and saying, 'But Sabrina went this way.'

When I went to recce my original first leg, from Moot Hall in Keswick to Borrowdale, I realised that the route Steve and Paul had both taken from High Rigg to Walla Crag crossed some non-open-access land. The line took a patch of farmland between the road at Dale Bottom and the open-access boundary line of Castlerigg Fell. There was another major alteration I had to make to the route for a similar reason and one that would cost me dearly.

TOP   Competing in the Modern Pentathlon Varsity Match for Cambridge University in pistol shooting and the three-kilometre cross-country run. © Zoe Rutterford, Chickney Hall Flowers.

BOTTOM   Adventure racing with Team Endurancelife in Godzone, New Zealand. © GODZONE, New Zealand.

TOP   Adventure racing. © James Kirby Photography.
BOTTOM   Spine Race. © Steve Ashworth.

TOP   Attempt two, day one, Haystacks. © Steve Ashworth.

BOTTOM   Attempt two, day five, Helvellyn. © Steve Ashworth.

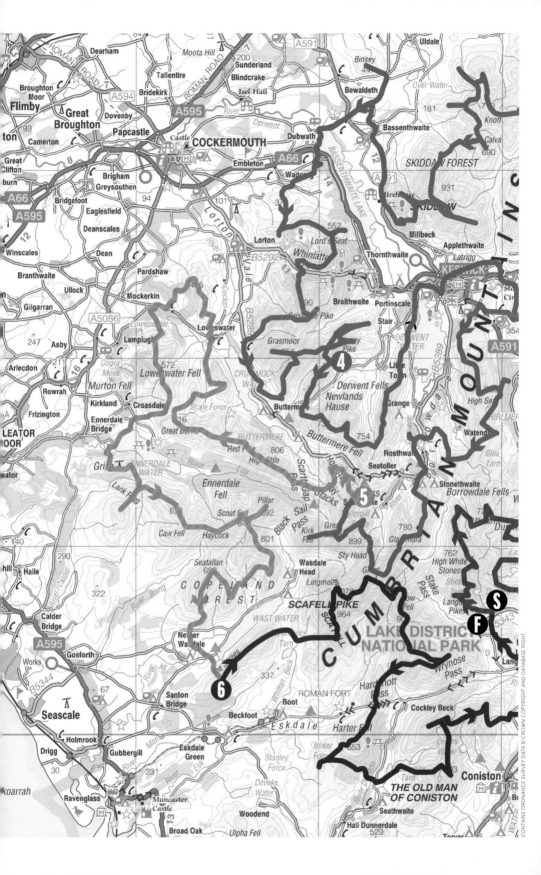

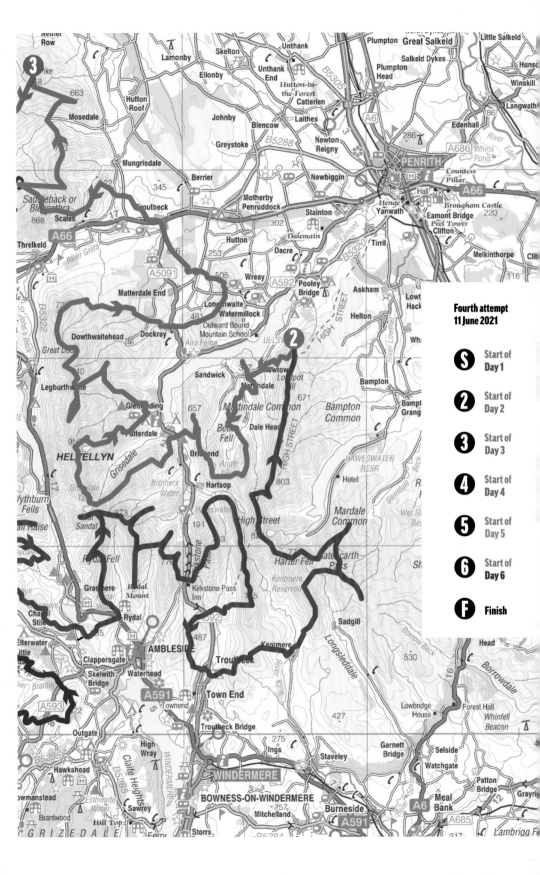

TOP LEFT   Ascending from Kirkstone with Mike Bottomley on the third attempt. © Steve Ashworth.

TOP RIGHT   Ben Turner and Steph Dwyer changing my socks while I have a cup of tea. © Steve Ashworth.

BOTTOM   Attempt three dawn on Mungrisdale with Peter Sowerby. © Steve Ashworth.

TOP   Descending Haystacks with Robin Bush on the fourth attempt. © Steve Ashworth.

BOTTOM LEFT   A very wet and cold Rannerdale to Newlands leg with Mingma Sherpa, Johnny Whilock, Tom Hare and Mike Robinson on attempt three. © Steve Ashworth.

BOTTOM RIGHT   With Rachel Platt on the fourth attempt. © Steve Ashworth.

TOP   The finish – greeting my husband at Sticklebarn after breaking the record (Johnny Whilock and Tory Miller in the background). © Steve Ashworth.

BOTTOM LEFT   Celebratory cake made by Maddy Wood. © Maddy Wood.

BOTTOM RIGHT   More cake at More Bakery in Staveley. © Ben Turner.

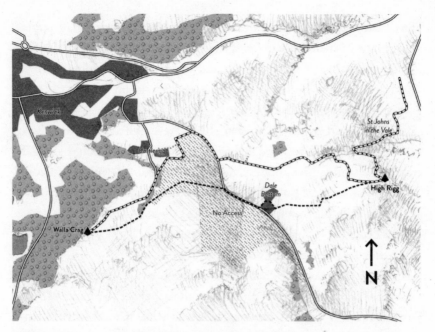

This map shows two routes. The northernmost is the way I took to avoid the private fields (not open access), and the more direct, shorter route below is the one taken previously.

Between Beda Head and The Nab, the route crosses Bannerdale Beck, which is surrounded by a boundary wall. The correct way to cross the river is to head to the southernmost point of the boundary wall, then follow it round and climb directly up The Nab from the west side instead of the northern nose, which is much gentler. To be honest, when I discovered this about the route I was a little shocked. I knew Steve would know all about open-access land. I also knew that Steve respected the Countryside Code. I suspect some of the finer detail such as this got lost in the grand scheme of plotting the entirety of a complicated route. In fact, perhaps I am impressed with how almost perfect the route truly was. I could certainly forgive this minor oversight.

Unfortunately, those following his route repeated the offence. Did no one else care? Had no one else noticed? Paul had wanted to beat Steve's record. So his tactic was to follow exactly the same route but run it faster, and that he did. It was an impressive effort and he shaved more than eight hours off, bringing the target closer to six days. It surprised me that even

Steve's same sequence on the Fairfield Horseshoe was repeated: dropping off from the Fairfield ridge at Great Rigg to traverse the rocky rubble of the western face of Fairfield to Seat Sandal and then re-ascending Fairfield. This was much less efficient than taking Seat Sandal on the way to Dolly-waggon Pike from St Sunday Crag.

I knew I couldn't run faster than either Steve or Paul, but there were other things I could be good at: managing sleep deprivation; being efficient; maintaining pace; optimising the route; and knowing that I could do it. I think this last point should not be underestimated. I didn't start any of my attempts thinking that I couldn't do what I wanted to achieve. I knew I had the staying power and the mental ability to just keep going. All I needed was for nothing bad to happen.

For me to complete the challenge within six days, I would have to do a number of things well. First, I'd need to endure the bare minimum of sleep. For fast runners like Joss Naylor, Steve and Paul, this might be a risky strategy. Their strength was their speed, and too little sleep could mean not enough recovery to maintain that speed. Even more risky was the effect that sleep deprivation could have on them psychologically. Any doubts about completing the challenge and there's a problem; sleep deprivation would only make that worse.

I would also need to be efficient. From my adventure-racing experience I knew I could be quick through support points and only do what was absolutely necessary while multitasking. For example, I could eat a meal while Ben changed my shoes and socks and I'd only change clothing when I really needed to.

Maintaining pace was crucial but I knew I didn't even have to think about my pace. I only really have one speed and I can do that for a long time: a very long time. Sure, it would start to degrade as the days ticked by, but not as steeply as for others, probably because I was starting from a slower speed to begin with. I also knew how to manage myself, to make myself eat and drink regularly. It was my experience that because I don't push my body quite as hard as other athletes, I don't typically suffer any gastrointestinal issues.

The final key factor was optimising the route. I had been totally dedicated to the challenge, and living locally meant I'd had the opportunity to recce

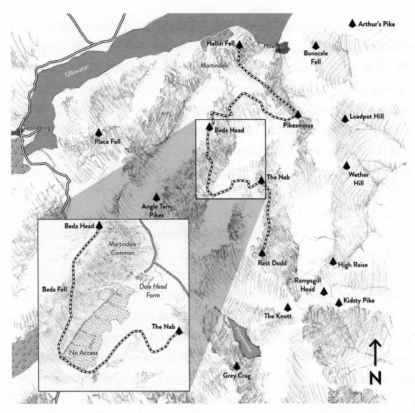

The route I took on the third and fourth attempts, using a similar route to Steve but extending the route to go around the non-open access land by running further south of Beda Fell around the wall boundary.

the route as well as building on my local knowledge. This meant I could scrutinise every option and make my own choices about which way to go and the order in which I would visit the summits.

After a few recces, I found an optimal line between High Rigg and Walla Crag that avoided the private farmland. This added about 1.5 kilometres and a little height gain. I also recced the direct line from Beda Head to The Nab a few times; it was a horrible steep descent, followed by an even nastier steep and quite long ascent, not a particularly attractive route option. So I did a major chop and change on the route and took The Nab out of that leg altogether. I had a couple of lovely runs from Beda Head along the ridge straight to Brock Crags. It was a beautiful way to go and so nice to avoid the awful up-and-down to The Nab.

However, as you learn when taking this route apart and putting it back together, for every gain there has to be a loss somewhere else in the puzzle. The Nab and Rest Dodd had then to be bagged at a different time, on the already very long leg from Kentmere to Martindale. Indeed, after visiting The Knott I would have to do a long out-and-back to Rest Dodd and then The Nab. I had already run the line from The Nab to Rest Dodd on a previous recce, and so after deciding that I liked the Beda Head to Brock Crags line, I never bothered to go back and recce this out-and-back to The Nab from Rest Dodd. Instead, I looked at the map and thought I would scope it out on the day. If there was a good line round the eastern slope of Rest Dodd that I could contour on the way back from The Nab to avoid revisiting the summit, then great, I'd take it.

It was frustrating that I had to make my route longer to avoid the non-open-access farmland Steve and Paul had cut through. I asked others what they thought and most of them wondered why I was troubling myself with it. They told me I should just do as the others had done because it was quicker. Paul and Steve had got away with it and so would I. But this was my point entirely. Doing things this way simply set a precedent for others to follow, like mindless sheep. I wondered why an organisation like the Fell Runners Association had not felt it appropriate to say something, but I knew I was in the minority. The majority of fell runners, it seemed to me, were far more interested in ensuring that all Wainwright attempts start at Moot Hall and less concerned with preserving the Countryside Code.

Not many of them thought it was important to get this right, but I could see a problem. I could see millions of dot watchers and avid Wainwright baggers looking at these tracks online. I could see hordes of fell enthusiasts charging through these poor farmers' land. My aim wasn't to do the Wainwrights Round in the fastest possible time at all costs. For me, the goal was to do it in a way of which I could be proud. If I could promote a way to do the Wainwrights and reinforce the Countryside Code, then I wanted to do it that way.

Perhaps it was appropriate that my stupid, self-righteous attitude ended up costing me the second attempt.

SEVEN

LEAN ON ME

I was exactly three and a half days into my second round when my route choice came back to haunt me. I was running with Simon Mills and Jacob Snochowski. We had started the leg only thirty minutes behind my six-day schedule. For the first three days I'd been more or less on target, but I'd had a bad night on the preceding leg, from Kirkstone to Troutbeck. The weather had been wet and windy and I had suffered a little from sleep deprivation. I found it desperately challenging to stay focused on the terrain around me because my head torch light kept bouncing off water droplets in the air. That was exhausting my concentration. During that leg I was with Dave Spence, who was navigating, and Paul Tierney, who was trying to keep me fuelled. It was a challenging night for them too; the conditions made things deeply unpleasant.

I decided we would take the ridge round from Hartsop Dodd to Gray Crag instead of bee-lining it across. I knew from my recces that the straight line was ten minutes quicker, but that had been in dry conditions during daylight. The descent was grassy but steep and in places rocky. In the wet, it would be slippery and treacherous as well as slow. Furthermore, we risked trouble crossing the river at the bottom, as it would be a lot higher at this time than when I recced it. The safer option of going round would be a

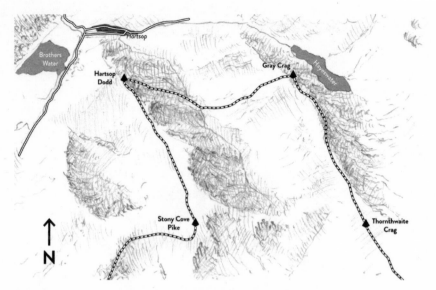

The direct route from Hartsop Dodd to Gray Crag taken in the fourth attempt.

great deal easier to navigate in these conditions.

Despite the logic, I remember feeling it was such a long way. This was because I was slow; I just found it so hard to keep my eyes open, and in that clag with the light just reflecting back into my tired eyes, not allowing me to see anything, it felt impossible, like delving blindly into a cave. Sometimes everything would suddenly go black because my eyelids had dropped like heavy shutters. But I was so tired it took my brain quite some time to realise this was why the lights had gone out. And so it went on – all night.

Ben was also having a bad night. Little did I know it but he was dealing with the consequences of my last-minute change in route that had sent the dot watchers into a mad frenzy. 'She's missed Stony Cove!' Poor Ben had a few worried phone calls at 1 a.m. and was on the point of heading out to find us and make us turn back to get it. Luckily he managed to get Paul on the phone, who confirmed we had intentionally missed it as we were going to do the out-and-back anyway.

Out-and-backs are a bit tedious. I desperately needed some stimulating conversation, but I had nothing to say to spark the chat and the boys were occupied. By the time we reached Yoke, I had lost the battle with my eyelids and knew I had to sleep there and then in the pissing wet rain and

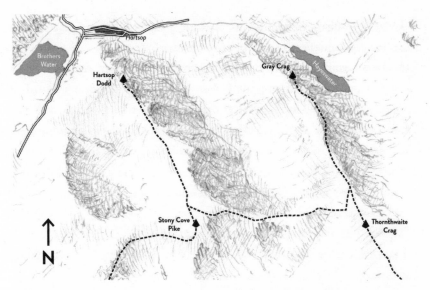

The out-and-back route used on the second attempt and by Steve, Paul and John Kelly.

chilly wind. So we put all my clothes on to keep me warm and I napped for some minutes before Paul-and Dave got me up. I felt a little refreshed but knew it wouldn't last. So while we continued, I suggested we call Ben to move the scheduled sleep stop from Troutbeck to the next road crossing between Troutbeck Tongue and Baystones. There I had a much-needed two-hour sleep in Johnny's camper van. It was a shrewd idea because if I had waited until Troutbeck I would have slept during precious daylight.

Comparing my schedule to my actual times shows how desperate I was for sleep. I should have arrived at Troutbeck Tongue at 3.01 a.m., but it was 3.50 a.m. when I actually got there, forty-nine minutes behind schedule. And yet, despite my two-hour sleep, I arrived at Kentmere at 8.33 a.m., only thirty-seven minutes down on my scheduled arrival time of 7.56 a.m. I made most of that time up by running quicker on Sour Howes and Sallows than my predicted times, clearly refreshed by some necessary rest.

Life on the support team was a whole other side to the story. My job was simple: put one foot in front of the other and keep going. Everyone around me, on the other hand, was rushing around in a frenzy, making sure everything I needed was in place. This was especially fraught whenever

I deviated from the schedule. Just moving a sleep from one place to the next had consequences for all the support team.

A classic example came on my fourth attempt. Even though I used timings from the third attempt (when I ended up ten hours ahead of schedule), I was still moving faster than expected when I reached Whinlatter. I remember arriving at the Visitor Centre to a very grumpy Ben. I had been quite happy, having just taken another twenty-five minutes out of the leg, but the first thing Ben said to me was, 'Where have you been?'

I was confused. 'I thought I made it round that leg in good time.'

'But you were at Whinlatter Top ages ago.'

'I know, but it's a long way down from up there.'

I was even more confused when he started complaining that I was going too fast.

'You're so far ahead of schedule, no one can come out and support you!' He seemed angry.

'So which is it, Ben? Do you want me to go faster or slower or stay here?'

I knew he was under pressure because moments like that are pretty rare from him. It was clear he was just very tired. He had been forced to shuffle lots of pacers around because some people couldn't make the new times I was hitting, pretty taxing on a person who had also been up for quite a few nights on the trot.

I think of Ben as the opposite of me. I'm impatient and a bit crazy, while he's patient and not prone to emotional outbursts. I'm probably quite an extreme personality; everything has to be done 'now'. That's why I like treating animals with an emergency. I know that I can act quickly and decisively when others might still be thinking about how to approach the task at hand. I often say to people, if you want something done now then ask me, but if you want something done perfectly in ten years' time ask Ben. I think we complement each other and work well together. The veterinary practice and bunkhouse are good examples. I have the ideas, the confidence and the audacity, while Ben is more calm and calculated. He can plot things out and visualise how something will be further down the line. He's a project manager and a really good one. He doesn't over-promise and always delivers, often exceeding what he's promised.

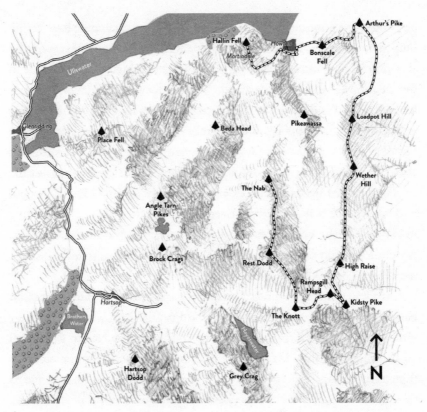

This map shows the adjustment I made to the route to visit The Nab after Rest Dodd, instead of from Beda Head as Steve had done.

Back on my second round, I'd reached the approach to Rest Dodd and asked Simon to go ahead and scout out the contouring line to see if it was any good. Meanwhile, Jacob and I headed up to the grassy summit. We met Simon again down the other side by the wall and he reported that the contour line had a nice trod and was doable. I pressed on to The Nab in sunny conditions. It was a lovely surprise to be met on the summit by Tory Miller, someone I would come to know very well through my Wainwright attempts, with a picnic of chips, tea and an avocado, cheese and tomato sandwich. The latter had become the staple food of the round, but I would find out to my cost a year later that I suffer from intolerance to avocados, the symptoms of which would soon be plaguing me.

After bagging the summit we turned back, descended back to the wall and followed Simon along the rocky trod to avoid re-ascending Rest Dodd. Due to the sharp angle of the slope, my right leg was higher than my left leg and after a few minutes I felt a pull in my right adductor on the inside of my thigh. This was the first niggle I remember feeling on my second attempt. I tried to ignore it but the burn got progressively worse. I stopped to stretch it a little, hoping this would relieve the pain, but if anything it did the opposite. I didn't really say anything to the guys but just struggled along, quietly wincing. The contour seemed endless. It gave me ample time to contemplate the consequences of my route choice, and I knew it would have been much better to go back over the top to save my legs. I was longing to get back to the ridge, where I could have both feet at the same height. My choice would cost me the round. In fact, my obstinacy about sticking to routes on access land had cost me the round.

According to my split times, I was pretty much on schedule for the first part of this leg. My time from Rest Dodd to The Nab was twenty-three minutes. Yet on the way back it took an hour from The Nab to Rampsgill Head, which is a little less than double the distance. Using the contour, there is much less relative height gain than going over the top, but due to the nature of the terrain it had taken a lot longer. On top of that, I had strained my right adductors and my right knee was starting to hurt. I had no real idea at this point of the damage I had done. Back on the grassy flat ridge, I was relieved to be out of agony and was able to break into a comfortable trot, but then my belly started gurgling and I needed to stop for the loo. Several times. Having finally got some momentum again, I was interrupted by my urgent gut motions, requiring frequent pit stops. Finally, at some point on the way to Arthur's Pike, I must have truly emptied myself, because I started to make more consistent progress. I even enjoyed the descent off Bonscale Pike despite the twinge in my right leg, which had also started to swell.

It's obvious that when you run, you use energy. But how you use that energy is critical on a multi-day challenge. In a short race, less than an hour, you can wholly rely on stored energy reserves. In fact, it's best not to eat because it's hard to digest food when you're running hard and anaerobically. We have two important body systems: the parasympathetic nervous system which promotes 'rest and digest', and the 'fight and flight' response of the sympathetic nervous system. When you run short and fast, your sympathetic nervous system is on and your parasympathetic system is off. When you run for days, you cannot rely on your stored energy. You have to keep yourself fuelled. Once again, there is a fine balance to be had between running so hard that you cannot eat, and eating so much that you cannot run.

While running the Wainwrights, I would have been burning anywhere between 300 and 600 calories every hour. It is impossible for the body to digest this many calories while running, so you have to anticipate an overall calorie deficit. However, it's important to try and get as much fuel in as possible, as much as the body can digest, which is around 300 calories per hour. My strategy when I run ultras is to try and eat 300 calories' worth of food in various forms: Mountain Fuel jellies, pizza, chocolate bars, cake and so on. I find it easiest if I trickle-feed this in, eating a small something every twenty minutes. So my ignorance of what avocados were doing to my guts was far from helpful.

Martin Stone was at Martindale and he joined us for a bit. As I threw myself off the side of Pikeawassa and thundered down the slope, he re-marked how surprised he was that I was still descending so well. Little did he know this was my response to the pain I was feeling. I'd kept it to myself as I mused about how much longer I was going to last. The fact I was hurting was probably the reason I was a little short with Tom Gibbs over his navigation. I was irritated at the bracken-infested line he had chosen, although I knew perfectly well it would be the optimal route. Tom is gifted in his navigational expertise and I trust him 100 per cent. He's also a close friend, so I guess I let my guard down and allowed my frustration to lash out.

Shane Ohly was the other pacer on this leg. Shane runs Ourea Events and is race organiser for the famous Dragon's Back Race. He's also a good friend and I was glad he was on this leg; he's always chirpy and encouraging. He had already suffered the misfortune of joining me on two legs back-to-back earlier in the round. Starting at Hard Knott Pass, he had the arduous job of trying to get me to eat. He knew how much I needed food and how little I was getting down. The only thing I would tolerate at that point was some of his vegan party-ring biscuits. They also cheered me up. Who doesn't love a party ring?

Despite not wanting to eat, I insisted on running as fast as I could. I was already ahead of my schedule and I knew I'd been quite generous on the split times for the leg.

I started that leg an hour and eighteen minutes ahead of my schedule and finished it an hour and twenty-two minutes ahead, a gain of four minutes. Those four minutes would cost me dearly. If I had just slowed down a little and eaten more food, the next leg would have gone considerably better. Instead, with an empty tank and heavy legs, I started up the long, steep, pathless slog to Dow Crag. Thankfully, Shane with his orienteering skills had found a better, more direct line than I had on my recces. Rob Bond had realised that no amount of coaxing was going to get solids into me, so instead he had encouraged me to drink a Mountain Fuel energy drink. He then cut the corner to Brim Fell, and Shane and I tackled the Old Man out-and-back while Rob got his stove going and made me some hot soup.

I'd only met Rob once before. He had asked to interview me after I'd raced the Spine and won the ladies' race. We got on really well and I mentioned my plans for the Wainwrights. He offered to help me on some legs. I really lucked out there. He had brought soup and baked some lovely cakes and tray bakes for me: how thoughtful! That warm cup of soup was the turning point. From feeling low, Rob's soup and the most beautiful sunset got me going again, and the three of us merrily trotted along the runnable ridge to Grey Friar with conversation restored, always a good sign for me.

Rob had been a great companion the night before as, buffeted by the wind, we groped our way in the darkness through Wind Gap to Pillar, fumbling for holds on the wet, slippery rocks. He shared my pain as I was swearing my way up the brutally steep, bracken-choked slope up to Middle Fell, another Tom Gibbs special. I couldn't hide how much I loathed this route. I was cross as well because I felt I was going slowly. We had started that leg an hour and a half ahead of schedule, but I miscalculated and thought we were losing time. Then, when we summited Seatallan a whole two hours and twenty-five minutes ahead of schedule and were treated to a long, grassy descent to Buckbarrow, all was forgiven. I might have overused the word 'sorry' to Tom. (Sorry, Tom.)

It's important to recognise the wonderful people I've been surrounded by. Of course, I hope I have been thoughtful and treated them well, but fear that in the moment, with fatigue and exertion, I've slipped up once or twice. I remember the scathing look I gave poor John Knapp when he gave me some delicious hot chips at Loweswater but had forgotten ketchup and mayonnaise. I nearly choked on one of them. Dr Knapp quite rightly just stood next to me not intervening, probably hoping I would choke to death for my ingratitude.

It was a relief to reach the summit of Beda Head and leave the bracken behind to run a beautiful sunny ridge over to Brock Crags. It felt quick because Tom and Shane were choosing fantastic lines, picking up little trods through the grassy bogs to the Angletarn Pikes. My right leg didn't hurt so much on flatter ground or up the rocky ascent to Place Fell. But as night fell, a vast dark cloud appeared, the heavens opened, the temperature plummeted and I clung on to Shane for support down the slippery wet rocks. Suddenly my knee was throbbing, but I didn't dare say anything. I knew we just had to get down as quickly as possible; it wasn't far to Patterdale, where the camper van was waiting.

The original plan was to sleep at the founder of Mountain Run Charlie Sproson's house in Glenridding after the next leg, but with the weather being so horrendous and it being 1 a.m., it made more sense to sleep where I was and sit out the worst of the weather. I was too tired to worry about the knee, just glad to rest my fatigued body and give in to heavy eyelids. After a two-hour sleep I was revived. I set off with Rob Bond and Giles Ruck, who I'd first met running the Yorkshire 3 Peaks ultra in 2019. We seemed to be moving up Arnison Crag well, beating my splits by a small margin. Even so, despite the sleep, I was still weary and the pain in my knee was exhausting. It wasn't so bad until I had to descend, but coming off Seat Sandal I realised how swollen my leg had become. I was having trouble bending it.

Up until then, I hadn't mentioned the injury to anyone else, but I was forced to let Giles in on the secret, although I think it was painstakingly obvious as I hobbled down to Grisedale Tarn, gripping his arm and wincing.

I was sure I couldn't go on like that; someone was going to notice how lame I was and make me stop. I mulled the situation over as I climbed up Dollywaggon Pike, while Giles and Rob seemed happy chattering away. Feeling sleepy despite the dawn light, I crawled over to a boulder and, resting my head on Rob's lap, I went to sleep. It was really cold and a bit damp, so I don't think I managed to sleep well or for very long before the shivering made me get up. My motivation had vanished. Was it all over?

Usually, it's spectacular crossing from Helvellyn to Catstye Cam along Swirral Edge. You're on a knife-edge ridge with a wide-open vista. Not that day. Shrouded in clag, there was nothing to see, nothing to inspire and no reason to go on. From the last summit of the leg, we bailed off the south side down to Red Tarn with me clinging to Giles in absolute agony. Arriving at Charlie's house in Glenridding, my first thought was to try to find someone to look at my knee and see if we could do anything to get it to a state where I could go on. I was just exhausted and collapsed on Charlie's sofa.

Ben sent Paul Tierney to come and see me. Paul looked at my swollen knee, although to be honest the whole leg was so swollen you couldn't make out which part was the actual joint. He decided it was simply acceptable wear and tear. I think because he had suffered on the descents, he felt I should too, and that this swelling was an acceptable consequence of the round. I should just get on with it and quit my moaning. What better person to give me advice than the man himself? *Excellent*, I thought. *That's what I needed. Someone to give it to me straight.*

It was strongly recommended to me by all involved that I should take some painkillers. I was unsure about this for a number of reasons. When I had been trialling for the GB squad in modern pentathlon, we were drugs-tested at random. I had always assumed you weren't allowed to take ibuprofen or have a large amount of caffeine, along with all the other contraband. I was also worried that ibuprofen could be damaging if taken while doing intensive activity. I knew that it was not good for my kidneys or my stomach if I was dehydrated, and there was certainly a risk that while doing this round there would be points when my hydration was poor. So I had wanted to avoid using these things. Even so, I was in quite a lot of pain and thought they might make things a bit easier. So I took some. But it still felt like cheating.

I started that leg two hours and thirteen minutes behind schedule. But I was still climbing well and held my split times all the way until Clough Head, which surprised me because the weather was atrocious and I felt I was very slow. Out of nowhere came another thick black cloud and we had a half-hour deluge. I got my handy poncho from Paul's vest pack and, despite it flapping in the wind, managed to get it on just in time. I might have looked ridiculous, but I felt rather smug as I remained bone dry.

It wasn't until the descent of Clough Head that my knee really began to trouble me. It was impossible to lift my unbending leg high enough over the grassy tussocks not to fall over. The only solution was to lean right over on my left side and throw my right leg out at an angle and so I grabbed on to Little Dave for support. 'Little' Dave Cumins is quite a character, often seen in the hills wearing a pink tutu or similar. He's very caring and also quite short, hence the name, and consequently helpful as a crutch to get me off the hill.

I didn't really think much of this beyond wanting to get off this miserable wet mountain and make it to the next support point to stop. When we hit the Old Coach Road, where I would normally have enjoyed picking up the pace, I was barely able to walk. I was sure my attempt was over, but became somewhat distracted by the joy of seeing Steve Birkinshaw and Chris Lines from Right Lines Communications walking towards us. No one seemed to notice the state I was in (maybe they had been warned); we just continued walking and chatting about other things.

At Dockray I sat down and iced my swollen knee; my whole leg was just getting bigger and bigger. I expressed my concern to Steve about whether I should go on, but it was clear he really wanted me to and suggested we just give it a try and see how we got on. I wanted to try my hardest for Steve. I didn't want to let him down. He had come to help me on the next leg and I knew he would look out for me. So I took more painkillers and continued.

Trying to run along the road was pitiful. I tried to push up Gowbarrow Fell and at one point exchanged a look with Steve and shook my head as though to say, 'This isn't working.' But on we went. Steve was very positive and told me that despite it all I was actually gaining on my splits. How could that be? I had allowed for a diminishing pace when I wrote the schedule, but I didn't think I had been *that* generous. Maybe this was how the round was done: very slowly. I reached Troutbeck only two and a half hours behind schedule. I had barely lost any time despite everything. Perhaps it really was worth carrying on and just seeing how it went?

My next support team, Joe Faulkner and Peter Sowerby, joined us on the next leg over Blencathra. I didn't want to follow Steve's route up the steep ferny gully on to Souther Fell. I had purposefully re-routed to zigzag the gentler sloping path and consequently added an extra kilometre, but Steve simply wouldn't allow me to go that way. I was too tired to fight. I just wanted to appease him and, after all, he was helping me out. Alongside Tom Gibbs, Steve is one of my navigational heroes.

It was late in the evening when we made the final descent into Mosedale. I had managed to move reasonably well until this point, but once again the long, steep, grassy descent challenged my swollen, unbending leg and so I linked arms with Joe Faulkner and used him as a crutch to get down. I arrived two hours and fifty minutes behind schedule.

I was excited to see my ex-adventure-racing teammate Jeff Powell Davies and fellow ultrarunner Howard Dracup. We rushed to set off up Carrock Fell before nightfall. As the night wore on, though, I really began to lose the plot. Sleep deprivation combined with the painkillers and my damaged knee twisted me into a babbling wreck. I don't remember too much, but at one point I woke myself up while I was still on my feet with the words, 'Let's paint the fences green.'

What fences? Why did they need to be green? I have no idea, but it made Howard laugh, so it was worth saying. There were a couple of moments when I was so much of a zombie I just collapsed in the grass, curled into a ball and went to sleep, a bad idea in the cold, wet conditions. I would then wake up shivering and need to move again. Progress was poor and by the time I reached Whitewater Dash I was over four hours behind schedule. The only thing keeping me going at that stage was the thought of my friends waiting for me at each of the remaining legs and I didn't want to disappoint them. So I just kept going.

It was a massive boost to see Mel Steventon, a friend I'd made on the Everest trip, bringing fresh conversation and encouragement on Skiddaw.

I had hardly eaten anything for a while and she had a hot flask of sugary tea. Perfect. She'd even brought a pot of custard, which because of its novelty was suddenly appealing. The rush of calories to my energy-deprived body allowed me to pick up the pace. I was with Sally Fawcett, a GB ultrarunner and sports physiotherapist, who kept encouraging me. We progressed well to Ullock Pike, but then I had to tackle the steepest, most technical descent on the entire round down Carl Side.

I didn't like this descent at the best of times. I stopped and looked down. How was I going to manage it? I couldn't go forwards. I tried a few things and don't really remember how, but in the end figured out the most comfortable and safest thing to do was to go down backwards and be guided by Jeff and Sally while holding on to their outstretched hands. It was bizarre and took forever, but eventually we were down. Then I climbed Dodd, the last little summit on the leg, before once again descending backwards.

The normally quick and gentle fire road that followed wasn't much fun either. My leg was throbbing and I was getting fed up of my disability. It was so annoying. I normally love descending and, unlike a lot of fell runners, I can hammer down hill after hill without suffering the effects of delayed-onset muscle soreness. That's how I managed to complete the Dragon's Back Race so quickly, by descending as quickly on day five as I did on day one. It was so frustrating to have one of my strongest abilities compromised. I resigned myself to a hobble and linked arms with Sally and Jeff to take the pressure off. I just wanted to get down and off the hill.

While we descended, Sally mentioned we shouldn't be seen like that. I asked why not. She said she had heard someone wasn't happy about it. I wondered what she meant. Why would me using a human crutch bother anybody else? I responded that to hide what I was doing would be dishonest, so I would carry on as we were and worry about that later. I can quite honestly say that I didn't give a toss what people thought about it. I just needed to get down that hill. In all likelihood I would have to stop at the bottom anyway. I couldn't imagine carrying on for another seventy kilometres like that.

At Dodd Wood car park there was cake: a perfectly baked Victoria sponge courtesy of Astrid Gibbs. I would have eaten the whole thing but sadly the legendary runner Wendy Dodds had beaten me to it. But there were two slices left, so I ate those. If there is one thing in my life that can motivate me to do anything, it is cake. Alas, it felt more like commiseration cake. I had invested so much time and energy to get to that point and yet was sitting in a busy car park swollen, fat, depressed, in pain, with cake crumbs all over me, in my dirty sweaty clothes. Not feeling like a proper, agile athlete was depressing. Was it all over? Despite the fact I had daylight, I crawled into the camper van to sleep. I would never have done that if I had intended to carry on.

When I woke, I was in even more pain. My entire body was swollen. My feet were so fat I couldn't get them in my shoes. All of me ached. It felt like I was bruised everywhere, and even a light touch on my shoulder was excruciatingly painful. Despite that, the team were still buzzing. Sally and John Knapp were ready and waiting to head up Binsey, and Ben had got my shoes and socks ready to put on.

'Really, guys? Do you want to crawl up and down the rest of the Wainwrights with me? It's going to be heinously slow and while I can manage to get myself up the hills, I'm going to need assistance to get down.'

'That's okay, we'll help you if you need it.'

'Well, okay then. Let's go.'

Sally wisely added, 'Let's just take it a step at a time. You can always give up later, but if you don't try you'll never know.' How right she was.

It wasn't easy to get going again. I couldn't put my own size 41 La Sportiva Mutants back on because my feet were too big. So I borrowed Ben's size 45 shoes. I looked ridiculous, clown-footing it along the busy main road to Bassenthwaite. Meanwhile, Ben was trying to source a size 41.5 from The Climbers Shop in Ambleside. At least it was sunny. And we found ourselves laughing at my predicament. In the end I took the huge shoes off and walked barefoot for three or four kilometres until Ben caught us up with the new shoes.

It's always hard to get going again once your body has shut up shop and started much-needed repairs. Even so, once you do get going, it does tend to improve and gradually the pain subsided. Oh, Binsey! You were just what I needed: a silly little hill but a great view nonetheless. I certainly didn't despise it, like Paul and Steve seemed to. Although the route along the road is quite boring, at least it's easy: there was no having to scramble over rocks and bash through bracken. My tired body appreciated a break from brutal ascents and tricky descents.

Arriving at the Pheasant Inn was a beautiful moment. So many friends were waiting for me in the glorious sunshine. I slumped into the chair Ben had put out and tried to engage in conversation with people I was so delighted to see, honoured that they had come out to support me. Chris Hope, Bruce Duncan and his dad and four jubilant pacers for the next leg: Mike and Hazel Robinson, Tom and Astrid Gibbs and three doggies. How could I not want to go on? Excited as I was, I still managed to fall asleep in the chair in front of this bubbling rabble, probably mid-sentence. I woke up drooling on my arm.

'You were snoring,' Ben said.

The next leg provided one of my fondest memories of the second attempt. We laughed, we joked and above all we moved. With such a special bunch of people, I completely forgot about my knee and any pain and just enjoyed the moment. Before I had time to contemplate how near the end I was, we had arrived at Whinlatter. And while I now had to tackle the shitfest of fallen trees, the heathery slope, the long steep slog, you know what? It wasn't as bad as I remembered. Tom Gibbs battled on in front with his navigational expertise and I chatted with Lou Osborn, who had joined us at Whinlatter. I didn't know Lou very well at that point but I knew she was a top-class fell runner. She had surprised me earlier by popping out to see me on Blencathra with her partner Paul Cornforth, and that really touched me. I had requested she join us on this leg and here she was: full of smiles and non-stop encouragement. I was so grateful.

It was a lovely evening and once up on to Grisedale I really enjoyed trotting along the bone-dry, rocky ridge with Tom, Lou and Ben. The descent off Whiteside was always going to be tricky, so I linked arms with both Ben and Tom and we scuttled down. Little did I know that keen dot watchers had decided something dodgy was happening. They judged my speed had increased, although I'm not really sure how. What were they comparing it to? I was still slower than my estimated splits. I had been very generous with the split for the descent off Whiteside, allowing for wet

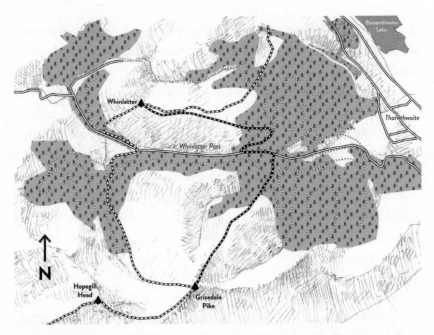

The two different route options from Whinlatter Top to Grisedale Pike. The route on the west side is that taken by Steve, Paul and myself on the second attempt with the support point in Hobcarton car park. The route on the east side is the one I took on the third and fourth attempts going via Whinlatter visitor centre. I found this route much more runnable as the other route involves climbing over lots of fallen trees and pushing through vegetation.

conditions that would have required far longer. Essentially, I'd used a worst-case scenario. There was apparently also some discussion that I was leaning on people in order to increase my speed to try and beat the record.

I didn't know all this at the time, but I find it both hilarious and inconceivable that anyone would think I would do that, not least because by that time the record was out of the window. I had known that since Dockray, if not before. And, to be honest, I hadn't been that bothered about the record in the first place. My goal of six days was likely unachievable from the moment I set off in flooded conditions. I'd already decided I'd be back the following year to do it properly. In addition, I wasn't going faster; I was moving staggeringly slowly. Indeed, looking back now, my split from Whiteside down to Rannerdale was one hour and six minutes on the second attempt, compared with thirty-nine minutes and thirty-six minutes on the third and fourth attempts. But clearly in dot-watching world there was a different story unfolding from what was actually happening on the ground.

At that point, although unaware of what comments were online or what anyone was saying, I had already come to the conclusion that my attempt couldn't be taken in serious contention for a record. But I was very much mistaken in thinking that in order to claim a record you had to register some interest first. I had assumed it was a bit like a race entry. When you enter a race you get a set of rules, and when you cross the line your position is recorded. When I decided to do the Wainwrights Round, I only knew of it as a thing that Steve did for a bit of fun. I'd thought the hard work and the skill had gone into the mammoth effort of designing the route. Running it was the icing on the cake. So when I decided to run it, I wasn't aware of any fixed rules about how it could be done and I wasn't sure why anyone would really care about me doing it. But that was before Paul Tierney broke Steve's record and it was all over the media as a massive deal.

Paul breaking Steve's record put the Wainwrights in the limelight. Now everyone was aware of it. It became a thing to try, and for some as quickly as possible. It would be a big deal if you broke the record. Yet that wasn't what attracted me to the challenge. It's true that I analysed the way that Steve and Paul had done their rounds. I broke each of their rounds down and worked out how long they had spent resting and running. In those respects, the two were very similar, so I guess in the final analysis Paul just ran faster than Steve. Both men are exceptional fell runners. Paul, being almost a decade younger than Steve at the time of his round, had an advantage. Endurance is something you gain from experience, and I do think that with a lack of longer races under his belt Paul had a well-worked-out strategy and bulletproof logistics that led to his successful one and only attempt. He had also put a lot of thought into how he would keep his muscles in good nick so he could keep running at a good pace. I remember him advising me that I should, like him, use professional physiotherapists and masseurs on my round as they were critical for maintaining the body.

When Paul stopped at our house in Langdale on his round, it was about 10.30 a.m. His masseuse had put out a couch and he lay on it getting a massage for a good half an hour. He stopped in at the house for a long time, and I knew I could save myself a lot of time not bothering with massages.

I wouldn't faff, I could sleep less and I would generally keep my stop times to a minimum. I knew I could run for a long time on very little sleep. I had a lot of experience of doing that, both adventure racing and working as a vet. Putting my schedule together, I reduced my sleep time to less than eight hours, compared to Paul's stopping time of around forty hours. It didn't surprise me that my schedule had me finishing in a quicker time. I would simply have more time to spend running; I could afford to run slower. Massages are just for elite runners, I told myself. In any case, I didn't know anyone who would want to follow me round the Wainwrights just to massage my aching legs.

Hobbling into Rannerdale, I chatted to Ben about the situation. He told me the two pacers on the next leg didn't want to give me any physical assistance. I was fine with that. I told him I was happy to go alone. I'd just take a race vest with the stuff I needed. In a way it would be easier because then I could go as slowly as I wanted. Part of the problem for me had been having pacers and then finding myself going so ridiculously slowly. It was embarrassing and I felt bad for taking up their time. I also thought it must be incredibly painful for them to watch me limp along. That was one of my reasons for accepting help; I just wanted to get a move on in whatever way possible so everyone could go home. Perhaps I should have just stopped? But it was clear no one wanted me to stop; they wanted me to finish the epic journey just as much as I did. I wanted to complete the recce. I wanted to get to Cat Bells: the last summit.

EIGHT
BROKEN

In dark, wet Rannerdale, I felt it important to make sure Nicky Spinks and Neil Talbott, my next two supporters, understood I had no wish to claim a record. I felt ashamed of the condition I was in and how slowly I was moving. They confirmed that they didn't want to physically assist me during the next leg. I was more than happy about that. I would rather crawl around alone with my self-pity and not have anyone watch me in such a decrepit state. Either way, I was going to stop to rest because I was no longer in any rush. It would be best to get some sleep, but not too much or my body would start to shut down for repairs. Then I'd never get going again.

After a couple of hours' sleep, I prepared myself to start moving once more. It was still cold, wet and dark and I felt a little depressed and deflated. I was now completely relaxed about getting to the finish. I would make it, but I was in no rush. Until Rannerdale, I had been pushing and pushing, not for the record but to save my support team the pain of crawling along at the speed my body really wanted to go. Now that everyone was on the same page with respect to the record, I could just mosey along. I double-checked with Nicky and Neil that they were sure they were happy about this arrangement, telling them that I was going to be very slow indeed and that I didn't mind at all if they preferred not to come with me.

That whole leg turned out to be quite miserable. Conditions were gloomy and drizzly and that was kind of how I felt. I struggled up to Rannerdale Knotts, fighting the bracken with my poles. I pushed up to Whiteless Pike, the biggest portion of climbing on the leg. I enjoyed the reprieve from the climb on the flatter, grassy slopes of Wandope and Grasmoor. Nicky and Neil were both extremely dutiful: they provided all the food, water and clothing I needed. Even when I was wearing a ridiculous number of warm jackets and complained I was still cold, Neil would conjure up another one. Looking back, I realise it wasn't just a question of being cold at all. My body was shutting down. I looked up at Crag Hill but was spent. I gave into fatigue, as I had lost the will to fight it. I stopped to rest. Nicky even got into the emergency shelter we had with us to keep me warm while I slept.

I managed to make an effort running down off Scar Crags as dawn brought new hope of a brighter day ahead. I struggled up to Causey and then we turned back to take the trod to Barrow, only we never found it and instead took a ridiculous line that was so thick with heather you couldn't see the hidden rocks or steepness of the ground. I knew it wasn't the right way, that it was slow and daft to persist with it, but I didn't really care. I let myself be tortured by the agony of trying to lift my stupid swollen knee and fat useless leg over the annoying spiky bushes. I allowed the spikes to scratch my hands and stab through my tights. Occasionally it was all just too much and I sat down to contemplate the situation.

Out of nowhere, Howard Dracup appeared. He was jubilant to have found us and started taking the piss out of me *and* my decrepitude. I laughed along with him and just like that I was having fun again. I can't remember when I first met Howard, but one day he announced that he was my Strava stalker; I think it was at a race we were both doing. I immediately took to him. He was honest, down to earth and a bit of a laugh.

Once we crossed the river and started heading up Barrow, the sun appeared and as I warmed up, my mood improved. Once again, I was hobbling along quite happily, counting down the final summits. The final descent down to Newlands was long and steep and I tried various ways to shuffle down the grass, but in the end I elected to sit in my waterproof trousers and slide down to the camper van. That was much faster than leaning on anyone, and also fun.

I had one short leg to go and six more summits. It had taken Paul less than three hours for this section, but I knew I could easily take twice as long with my leg the way it was. Since I was no longer in any hurry, I decided to have a good sleep there in broad daylight. Then I started again. That last leg took me almost eight hours, but looking back it was one of the best. I was with friends and we were all joking and laughing. I hiked up Robinson well at the start, still able to climb with some speed, but the descents were terrible. I had also developed a serious water retention issue. When I measured my weight at the finish versus my weight at the start, I must have been carrying at least eight and possibly ten kilograms of fluid. My legs had been swollen for some time and had lost all definition. Now I was retaining water around my abdomen. As we started that leg, we joked I looked nine months pregnant. By the end, I joked with Howard that I was expecting triplets.

After an ultra, most runners experience some fluid retention. It's debatable why exactly this happens but it is likely a combination of factors. Sodium levels in the blood are reduced from sweating. There's a lack of venous return caused by not lying down; subjecting blood flow to extended periods of gravity can increase the leakiness of valves that would normally stop the back flow. Normally this is associated with standing up. When you run, muscles should help squeeze-return the blood, but it's possible I was going too slowly for this to have much effect. There are hormonal reasons too, particularly increases in cortisol as a result of stress on the body. Finally, injury causes inflammation and this can also result in fluid build-up. I think all of these factors were affecting me; the knee injury made everything that much worse.

As I waddled along the ridge, I wasn't thinking about my swollen, sleep-deprived body or my painful knee. All I was thinking about was the last summit. I remember the sun shining so strongly, and as I started that final ascent to Cat Bells I could hear Johnny Whilock playing the bagpipes. I became overwhelmed with joy and a huge sense of achievement. I had made it. I threw my arms in the air and soaked up the atmosphere of the little crowd that had gathered to celebrate my round.

The one real regret I have about this second attempt is wishing I had called time at Cat Bells. I suggested this to Martin Stone as a clear-cut way of showing that I was not claiming a record. But everyone else was of the opinion that I should complete the round and carry on to Moot Hall. I didn't want people to think that I couldn't make it to Moot Hall and I also wanted to please my support team; they had all worked so tirelessly to support me and I wanted to complete the round for them. So on we went.

The sun was glowing and I was so happy. I'd had such a fantastic week with amazing friends. But it was a long slog along the roads of Portinscale and I was feeling the weight of all that retained fluid on my exhausted body. Finally, I passed through the streets of Keswick, unusually quiet even for a Sunday, thanks to the pandemic. Mustering all the energy I had left, I broke into a little trot up the Moot Hall steps. Thankfully, there was only a tiny gathering to welcome me back. (I'd been keen to make sure we did not cause a Covid-19 outbreak and so had asked on the dot-watching page for people to kindly refrain from going there.) Even so, I was truly delighted to see Steve Birkinshaw and Joss Naylor there to cheer me in. Sitting on the little bench having a natter with Joss remains one of my fondest memories of finishing, despite being so tired that all I wanted was a bath and some food and to go to bed.

I had failed to finish in less than six days, but I was delighted to have completed my journey around all the Wainwright summits. It didn't matter to me that things had all gone a bit wrong; that I had injured my knee and leant on people. I had known before I even set off that it would not be my record-breaking attempt and that I would do it again the following May. So it didn't occur to me at the time that my round, completed in six days and eighteen hours, would be newsworthy. I also wrongly assumed that people had to declare themselves a record holder, and this I never did. I just scuttled off home quietly to catch up on my much-missed sleep.

It's Monday morning, or something like that, and I'm doing a good impression of the newest Teletubby: 'Sabs', the broken, brown one. My phone is ringing. Was ringing. Is now pinging texts. I'm awake, I'm asleep ...

I need water ... I need painkillers. I'm in a pile of drool and a wet bed. The sheets are wet from sweat; I still have bladder control, thankfully. That's about all that I *can* say for myself. I need to get up. No, that hurts, I need to lie down.

Right, I'll just stay here for now and read these messages. The phone is ringing again. It's a man from a newspaper who wants to interview me. I chuckle.

'There is no chance of me going anywhere today,' I tell him.

'That's okay, I'll come to you.'

'Sure.' I laugh, thinking he has no idea where I live. So I give him my address, expecting him to say it's too far, or he doesn't know where it is.

Instead he says, 'Is it okay if I come in an hour? Do you want me to pick anything up?'

'Erm ... can I call you back, please? Because now is not a good time.'

A lot of pretty basic thoughts are going through my head. *Am I going to be able to get out of this bed? Am I going to be able to put clothes on? Is a shower possible?* I'm really quite crippled. Every move takes careful planning. Let's start with this, *Sabs: try and roll on to your front. Okay. Next, swing a leg out of the bed. How painful is it to touch the floor? Right, brace yourself.* I'm up – sort of. My feet are weirdly numb and so swollen it feels as though my skin is con-stricting my blood supply. My legs are like frying sausages when you forget to prick them; they're about to explode. Fuck! I need a Zimmer frame.

Come on, Sabs, you really need the loo. But there's a decision to make. There's a small one six feet away but it's a tight space and too difficult to manoeuvre. The main bathroom is further but easier to navigate. I start shuffling. *Okay, this isn't impossible.* I make it to the big bathroom. But now that's done I feel ravenously hungry. *Fuck's sake, why is our kitchen upstairs?* Well, I'm not getting dressed. I grab my phone and anything else I might need, because I'm not coming back. Right, I can do this. But the cat's in the way. Missed you, puss cat; would love to stroke you but you're much too far away, down there on the ground. And I'd really appreciate it if you would not trip me up while I spend the next few minutes negotiating this staircase one step at a time.

Looking from the outside, you might assume I recover easily or skip this stage altogether. This is absolutely not the case. Every recovery has been a learning experience. I can enter an ultra in prime condition, feeling lean and fit, and at the end I'm a swollen, crippled mess. It is possible to minimise the mess and swelling but, like most things, prevention is better than cure. After the Winter Spine, I took a long time to recover because I wasn't at my fittest on the start line and during the race I sprained my ankle, causing more inflammation and swelling than if I'd been fit and injury-free. Our bodies are incredible and they try to repair the damage we do to them, but it does take its toll.

This was also my experience with the knee injury on the second Wainwrights attempt. Once I've pushed through an injury and done more damage but finished the challenge, there is an extended recovery period and at this point there isn't a lot you can do to speed it up. The body just needs time. You can help it along in the right direction by resting, getting plenty of sleep, icing swollen bits, gentle massage to help flush things through and later on more skilful and directed healing with a physiotherapist or sports-massage therapist. But a speedy recovery can only happen with an injury-free race. After my third attempt, my legs recovered quickly and I was running well within three weeks because I hadn't injured myself. That allowed me to run the fourth successful attempt six weeks later. I've also found it's important to eat well while running. Even after a few hours of running, if I've not eaten well I find it harder to recover. The right food is also important: something that's easy to digest and mainly carbohydrate with some electrolytes (salts) to replace those lost from sweat.

Upstairs in the kitchen, Ben is on a call, working from home.

'Morning, darling,' I say. 'Do you want a cup of tea?' I ferret around the kitchen. The fridge is decidedly bare and I have a sudden craving for bread and of course we don't have any. I forage around, eating pretty much anything I find, like a hoover.

'Have you made my tea yet?' Ben's talking and I realise I've fallen asleep, apparently mid-mouthful because there's still something in there. Okay, let's try that again. Boil the kettle. I did that already. Get cups. Tea bags. Milk. Ooh, there's cheese in the fridge. I'll have some of that.

'Tea?'

Ah. Yes. Let's get the milk. That's why I'm still here with the fridge door open.

'Here's your tea, honey,' I say proudly. 'Do you think I should speak to a man from the paper?'

'Which paper?'

'I have no idea. I thought it might be a good way to get the message out about this not being a record. What do you think?'

The phone rings again. I'm going to assume it was the same man from the same newspaper but I can't be sure. He does definitely want to come and see me at Langdale, though.

'Remember you offered to pick something up? Please could you grab a loaf of bread?'

'Of course!' He seems willing. Maybe it is the same guy. 'Is there anything else I can get you?'

'I don't suppose you could get some cake?'

I have to admit I can't remember the finer details of the days that followed. I did some interviews. Somehow I shuffled over to the New Dungeon Ghyll Hotel, where I was filmed outside under a shelter put up for the pandemic. Whatever I was wearing was chosen because the clothes were easy to put on, not because they made me look good. I thought I was doing an interview for a newspaper, so the camera was a surprise. I told the reporter I had a message to get out. It was important everyone should know that I had received physical assistance during my round and so what I had done didn't count as a record. It was a bit like the blind leading the blind, as semi-comatose I tried to explain what I'd done. It sounded like a confession and the reporter became confused. Had he wasted his journey?

'Did you climb all the Wainwright summits?' he asked.

'Yes.'

'Did you visit them all on foot?'

'Yes, but I had to lean on people to get down the hills, so it doesn't count.'

'Why doesn't it count?' He was insistent that I was the first woman to summit all the Wainwrights in one go and that it didn't matter if I had leant on people to descend. He didn't get it and I was far too tired to put forward any coherent argument.

'I'm going back to bed now.'

I still have no real idea what exactly went out in the media about my second attempt. I was too tired to watch the news and read the papers at that time. I got the sense my message about the record wasn't getting through. That concern made me write to Neil Talbott, the secretary of the Fell Runners Association. I took the chance to thank him once again for his help, not just on the hill but also for his advice about the weather and everything else. He really had been amazing. But I wanted to explain my position.

'I know it will be bothering you about this downhill assistance and I've tried to deal with it as best I can,' I told him. 'I've just been honest with the media. Unfortunately they seem to not care and edit out the bits where I mention it! I have no problem if the FRA are unhappy about the way in which I completed the round: they cannot "ratify" it as it were or stamp some kind of authority on it. Personally, I feel that I completed the whole round on my own efforts assisted by my support team. If I had been chasing a record and we were looking at minutes/seconds making a difference, then I would have been more mindful of the help I was receiving. Unfortunately, I cannot do anything about this now and need to move on. I've decided to attack this again in May 2021. I'll put a proper women's record down, then we won't have to worry about this attempt anyway.'

Neil's response was a little unnerving. 'I think I do need to let you know that I've been contacted by several people, both as "supporter Neil" and "FRA Secretary Neil", about the nature of the attempt.' Clearly the issue of 'downhill assistance' on my Wainwrights attempt was a hot topic. 'So far I've just batted this off, but I can't keep on doing that (at least as FRA Neil). It is likely, I think, that the FRA will be asked for an official comment soon. I am really sorry this even needs discussing when you have done something unprecedented and extraordinary. However, it is obvious to me that enough people are aware of the issues that everyone will know soon enough.'

It was clear that this thing I did (and I still hadn't quite comprehended exactly what it was I had done) needed to be publicly unclaimed as a record to satisfy the FRA. I still felt confused at why everyone was so invested in it. I hadn't claimed a record. I didn't want a record. Wasn't that enough? Who were all these people? I continued to get texts and messages of congratulations and I didn't really know what to say. Saying something like 'I didn't do anything' seemed ungracious. But I really wasn't happy at all. I certainly hadn't done my best. I knew I was capable of getting round in a much better state not crawling round like a lame duck, leaving aside the embarrassment of my general state (Mr Blobby's wife). Now, literally adding insult to injury, I was being accused of trying to cheat? Oh my god, please could the ground swallow me up whole?

I continued to get loads of messages of congratulations, every one of them a stabbing reminder of the mess I was in. I couldn't be happy about the round. I didn't want to be congratulated, not because some people out there had decided I cheated by leaning on people, but because I didn't succeed. The original plan had been to run round the Wainwrights in fewer than six days. So why does it matter what I did on my non-record-breaking hobble around the Wainwrights?

Neil is a wise man and a good friend, so his view gave me pause for thought. 'If you choose not to say anything, given the issues are widely known about already, I think it would be on the cusp of appearing underhand. This would bring a serious risk of reputational damage within the fell-running world (completely irrespective of any FRA position or comment), which is something I really do not want to see happen.'

At that point, I just wanted to disappear into thin air. Instead, I needed to make yet another public statement about a thing that I was trying to let just fizzle out. I had tried that with the journalists I'd talked to and that hadn't worked, judging by the fact I was still getting messages of congratulations.

So I decided to write a statement that could not be adulterated by the media and publish it on a fell-running online forum. What better place to address the people who this would matter to the most? But I felt like a naughty schoolgirl standing in front of the classroom repenting her sins. The title of the post was: 'It's not a record'. I couldn't be clearer than that.

I explained how I had set off with a schedule that would beat the record, but how my knee became injured and my pace fell, and about needing to lean on someone. And how I was committed to finishing anyway.

'I did what I needed to do,' I wrote, 'had my knees strapped up and took some painkillers and struggled on through the rest of the summits. However, there were other points that I required assistance: I had to descend backwards down Carl Side to Dodd Wood and to do this I held on to two supporters to guide me down between the rocks. There were a few more descents where I had to lean on my supporters and I think this allowed me to descend far quicker than I would have on my own. I visited every summit and made the entire way on my own efforts with every step taken by myself. But having to lean on supporters to descend is not appropriate for taking a record. I certainly would not have tried to claim another's record by using these methods.

'I completed the Wainwrights Round to my own satisfaction but I do not wish my attempt to be ratified or acknowledged by the FRA or any other claiming some right to the Wainwrights. I do not claim any record for this achievement. However, I do look forward to taking on the challenge again in the future.'

It felt like an unburdening of the soul, even though my main motivation for speaking out was to please Neil. I felt so terrible that I had upset him. I hadn't meant to disrespect the rules, largely because I hadn't realised there were any. But there were clearly some ruffled feathers out there. I didn't really get it. If I have a problem with someone or something they've done, then I speak my mind to them about it. They have a chance to explain and then we both get over it. Making snide comments to third parties seemed unhealthy to me. It would take another nine months before I found out what the real problem was. It wasn't that I had leant on people as such. It was that I had dared to think that I could break a man's record and that I had almost done it. There could only be one explanation for this imposs-ible feat: I must have cheated.

Could a woman break a man's record? Of course she could. In fact, she already had. In January 2019, Jasmin Paris showed the world that a woman could win the Winter Spine Race outright, and not only that but could simultaneously provide breast milk for her young baby. What made the performance even more extraordinary was that she shattered the course record by twelve hours. She also set a fastest known time for the Ramsay Round in Scotland, man or woman.

It's a complicated subject, but one thing I can say for sure is that women are not faster than men. But they can be smarter. Is that sexist? Is that politically incorrect? Some might think so, but really it's just common sense. Some men are smarter than other men. Why can't some women be smarter than some men?

The Pennine Way is 268 miles and, although it has signposts dotted here and there, it is not straightforward to navigate. Before entering the race, I think most women would make some attempt to get to know the route so that on race day they wouldn't have to rely only on their navigational skills. Are some men more complacent perhaps with their approach to races? Do they more readily enter something more challenging? Perhaps also women can be more open-minded, ready to admit ignorance, thereby identifying key skills that are needed for the task at hand and doing what they can to prepare themselves for a more successful adventure.

What's more, 268 miles is a long way: the winter and summer records for the race are around eighty hours. That's over three days. You're clearly going to need some sleep, but how much? That's up to each individual athlete to decide. Every precious second spent sleeping is a second of race time lost, but if you have too little sleep you end up blundering around like a zombie and that can be even more costly in time. Lose your way and you can end up wasting precious minutes on tired feet wandering helplessly in the wrong direction. I understood that very well from my Summer Spine experience in 2019 when I only realised I was heading back the way I'd come when I spotted a piece of yellow pipe for the second time. I'd fallen asleep at the wheel and turned myself around. Ouch! My tired body did not appreciate that mistake. I wasted half an hour, time I could have spent in a sleeping bag.

It's not just sleep you have to manage on these endurance events; there are other tactics involved. In the Spine Race I have seen at least one racer use the tactic of following a slower runner who knows the course. Staying in company can be a good tactic not only for staying awake – as you can talk to each other – but also for ensuring you're going the right way.

In addition to going in the right direction and staying awake long enough to maintain efficient forward motion, you also have to look after yourself. In the depths of winter this is particularly important. You might assume that women feel the cold more than men, and are consequently more at risk. Yet women are also, generally speaking, more risk-averse than men, and so more likely than men to pack a set of extra insulated layers. While Jasmin Paris was running to victory in 2019, Eugeni Roselló Solé had to call it a day at Hut 2. My heart bled for him, as I am sure it did for many thousands of dot watchers, seeing him pull out so close to the finish, but it was a consequence of hypothermia, a problem that might have been avoided. There's always a balance between speed and self-preservation.

Next there's the faff factor. I'll not name and shame, but having raced with various combinations of three men in an adventure race, I have seen all kinds of faff. I have watched a man take half an hour to pack his rucksack at a transition. And then, as we were about to leave, he tipped all the contents on the floor and started again. I have seen it all: the body slumped in a chair, the eyes staring into space, the mind on walkabout from sleep deprivation. This happens to women too, of course, but we don't have a physical disadvantage that prevents us from being competitive when it comes to sleep. Put all these factors together – self-preservation, navigation, sleep deprivation and so forth – and the truth starts to emerge: the longer the race, the less important the running is.

Men will always be capable of running faster than women, so the fastest woman will never be faster than the fastest man. This is to do with the physical attributes that define our sex: darn those childbearing hips. It is a minor miracle that any bipedal could give birth; the two do not go well together, making us women an evolutionary compromise. To be bipedal we must suffer the existential risk of childbirth, still a dangerous activity even with all the luxuries of modern medicine and technology. Lovely strangers send me wonderful messages when I'm racing, but I congratulate all women who have given birth. That's something I could never do. I'm not brave enough.

I'm in danger of becoming a strident feminist, which I'm not. Women have fine attributes, but men do too. We are different. I get fed up with people trying to make out we're the same: we just aren't. I have been asked if there should be an overall Wainwrights record for both sexes. I personally don't care but for those women who want to win races and records, why on earth should they have to fight against men? Women are literally disabled from their childbearing hips, their higher body-fat percentage and different muscle structure. Trust me, there's a disadvantage. So please can we reward women and men separately but equally?

I have had some statistics thrown at me, but the truth is that the data is lacking. Let's say the advantage is ten to twelve per cent. You arrive at this figure comparing the fastest man and woman over a particular distance: ten kilometres, the UTMB, the Spine Race and so on. The larger the field, the more credible the result is. Things get a bit skewed with so few women ultrarunning. I think the problem is that the few of us that do it happen to be quite good.

To be honest, it was only a matter of time until a man broke the Wainwrights record. Sometimes it's just a case of the faster men not having tried yet. However, I really don't consider myself to be a fast fell runner. I don't turn up to short fell races because it would be an embarrassment – no one believes me, but if I turn up I'll either be wrong or I'll embarrass myself. I did actually do the Pike o' Blisco fell race – the Blisco Dash – as it starts very near my house. I only did it once! I was last, but bizarrely won six beers for my efforts. The winner only got one. So when we compare Paul Tierney, a renowned fast fell runner, with Sabrina, a good ultrarunner, Paul wins on speed every time. I did not run the Wainwrights faster than Paul. I didn't run the Wainwrights faster than Steve, and I sure as hell didn't run the Wainwrights faster than Joss. I was just like the tortoise that raced the hare in Aesop's famous fable. The hare leaves the tortoise behind and, confident of winning, takes a nap midway. On waking, he finds that his competitor, crawling slowly but steadily, has arrived before him. It was all the other things that are not running that made the difference for me, especially sleep.

Or, as Paul Tierney put it, I'm 'one tenacious little fucker'.

My plan was to keep moving, slowly and surely, in the right direction, minimising my stops as much as possible. On the second attempt I had tried to scrimp on sleep too much, pushing sleep deprivation to the brink of what is humanly possible. I realised that a little more sleep would be required to crack the six-day boundary. The statistics for my successful run say it all. Paul's moving time was about 110 hours, so his average was around 4.75 kilometres an hour. My moving time was 132 hours, so I was averaging four kilometres an hour. That really is quite a lot faster: twenty per cent faster. I had to make up for this lack of speed in other ways. Paul spent around forty hours not moving, whereas I spent less than twelve hours not moving. Not all of those hours were spent sleeping, but you can see the difference.

Food was also important. On the second attempt I ate too many fatty and fibrous foods that my body couldn't digest, in addition to the avocados I later found out don't agree with me. I'm distraught because I love them. I also realised timing was really important. The best conditions are when the bracken is low, the temperatures are stable, it's not too cold or hot, and there is a good amount of daylight to make the nights shorter. It's harder to navigate in the dark and harder to fight sleep deprivation, which is also a problem in the heat. So I wanted to go in May. I would learn on the third attempt that May is not reliable enough. Indeed, you can get snowed on. History shows that the majority of record-breaking attempts happen in June. Patience is important. There's no need to rush into a Wainwrights attempt if the weather is too windy. There was much I still had to learn.

'I think you're stark raving bonkers nuts to want to do this again,' Neil Talbott told me. 'But it would certainly resolve the issue once and for all.'

NINE
THIRD TIME LUCKY?

My creativity is both disruptive and annoyingly predictable, with no respect for my need to sleep. It waits quietly until I'm perfectly comfortable and about to drift off into that restorative paradise I so often struggle to reach, at which point my mind fills with a chaotic explosion of ideas that have to be recorded on paper at once for fear they are lost to the void forever. Which would be a shame.

So I lie as still as I can, trying not to disturb my husband, who is snoring peacefully. And I try to ignore these thoughts and go to sleep. I must not worry about losing them. I will remember them in the morning. It is not necessary to leap out of bed right now and grab my laptop and start typing out the contents of my mind. They can wait. I can wait. Sleep is refreshing. Sleep is important.

But I can't. I'm still the undisciplined, unruly child who won't go to bed. So I get up and I write. I write until I have unburdened myself of the stories in my head. Not the bit of the story that ought to be written next, but the bit of the story I had not yet contemplated or even acknowledged needed writing. That sparks off new ideas that fly out so fast I don't catch most of them.

At other times I try to prove to myself that I do have some sense of discipline. I can conform to the norm if I want to, right? So I have breakfast and sit down at my desk and try to be organised. I read through the bits of the book that I've just written and have a think about the gaps that need to be filled. Then I concentrate and write that bit of the story in a logical and systematic way.

That's boring, though, isn't it? Who wants to read that? I think about how magical it is when the words just come floating out of me because when they hit the page in a beautiful flow, then they read in much the same way and give joy, even if they don't necessarily have purpose.

That's how I think about my running sometimes. It felt like a delightful burst of freedom, setting off on my third attempt on a chilly morning with John Kelly, Ben and Darren 'Dazmo' Moore. We charged up to the first summit and – boom! – just like that, Loft Crag in thirty-six minutes: a personal best. *Should I be doing this kind of thing on a Wainwrights Round that's going to take six days? Should I impose some self-discipline? It's far too much fun!* My husband was muttering under his breath that I was going too fast and I was relishing the thought that I might just make John Kelly break a sweat.

This third attempt started on 30 April in the precise conditions I wanted: the ground was solid and bracken-free; it hadn't rained for a few weeks. It was a bit colder than I would have liked but that didn't worry me so much. Best of all was my physical condition and, boy, was I psyched. I was so fit and ready for this challenge. I had come out of winter already fit and spent the spring months topping up my speed with more and more recces, conditioning my legs to the hills.

So I wasn't going to slow down. I was going to dance along the summits and I was going to hang on tight for the ride. At Eagle Crag I indulged John with a brief pose on the summit for his camera. Dazmo had to head back to Langdale, but the three of us pressed on. The weather was improving and the mist was lifting, confirming that this could be it: lucky number three. Ben knows the intricate trods best, but he was struggling with the pace, so I took my chances and let my feet run away with me down the steep grassy bank to the river before the long slog up Ullscarf.

Except it wasn't a slog; it turned out to be easy. The sun was trying to burn through the mist and I was eating and drinking well but we were out of water. The boys stopped to refill and I charged on alone down Cat Gill and through the mossy bog towards Steel Fell. It felt great, the ground was drier than usual and I almost made it to the summit before John caught me up. Calf Crag, Gibson Knott and Helm Crag: I know this ridge well. It's the same route on Wainwright's Coast to Coast, which I'd run on Boxing Day four months earlier.

That's a gentle reminder of how much I put myself through in 2020. The Winter Spine Race in January. The first Wainwrights Round attempt in June. The second attempt in July. The Pennine Way FKT in September. And finally the FKT for the Coast to Coast in December. It was a lot. As Martin Stone put it: 'The thing that makes Sabrina extraordinary, more extraordinary than anyone I know, is the things she's done this year. And can you imagine anyone else on this planet who could do all of that and then come back and make another attempt on the Wainwrights in less than ten months?'

At Helm Crag I recalled climbing up on the second attempt to meet Wendy Dodds, who brought some refreshing goodies. And Howard Dracup on the summit with my Uber Eats order. I had fond memories of this little hill on the Coast to Coast too, with Mike Bottomley leading the way and the hand of Storm Bella shoving me along rather forcefully. I was gobsmacked to meet Scott White up there with Phraoig, his collie, because I knew he must have pushed through one hell of a headwind to reach us and it was freezing and very wet. What a night that was! Hailstorms, gale-force winds with gusts of eighty to ninety miles an hour blowing us over, icy puddles and seahorses on Grisedale Tarn. I'd never seen anything like it. It was terrifying, mesmerising, exhilarating and exciting all at once. It was beaten only by the next leg from Patterdale up to Kidsty Pike, which was, according to Ben, 'exceedingly dangerous'. I loved it! How can you ever feel more alive than when the elements are doing their damnedest to throw you off this Earth and you are winning? The more the wind blew, the more I charged up that hill. Ben wanted me to sack it off and turn around. 'To hell with going back,' I shouted. 'At least the wind is behind us, taking us where we want to go, even though it is throwing me on the ground occasionally. I'm not going to go into that headwind.' Not that he could hear me. The wind was too ferocious for any form of conversation. It took all my energy to hang on to my hat and head torch.

Poor Ben. He's always getting caught up in my mad, adventurous plans. Now he was here with me again on my third attempt at the Wainwrights, bombing off the side of Helm Crag down the steep and thankfully bracken-less trod. He left John and me to summit Tarn Crag as he caught his breath and navigated ahead towards Codale Tarn. It was Blea Rigg next but we'd run out of water again. I pressed on and John caught me up. Then it was Silver Howe, Loughrigg Fell and the steep, winding descent to Rydal.

Leg one had taken less than six hours, definitely the fastest I'd ever run through this section. I was so excited and energised that I didn't want to pause at the support point at the Badger Bar in Rydal, where Debs was eagerly waiting in her support role with the pacers for the next leg. Instead, I just carried on and started up Rydal Mount, explaining to the current team that I'd start heading up to Nab Scar when they diverted to the pub to finish their leg. I left it to them to explain to the new pacers that they would need to catch me up.

Naturally, that confused the support team and pacers, but they all went along with my mad plan. Paul Tierney, Tom Gibbs and John Kelly all caught me up. Tom was grumpy. Why was I early? He'd left the car park in such a hurry that he hadn't shut the door to his car and he'd forgotten his hat and gloves. I felt bad. It was going to be cold. In fact, I do believe snowflakes were already falling. I couldn't offer him anything. I was myself already dressed in John's hat and gloves, while mine were somewhere buried deep within the Tardis that was John's tiny running vest. They were tucked away so compactly that he didn't dare get them out or else the bag would explode. He handed me his more accessible clothing as I requested some layers.

'Burger, bacon, brie, baguette,' said Tom. 'If you want anything beginning with b, I've got it.'

'Thanks, Tom. I'll have the prawn and Marie Rose baguette. Who's got that one?'

'I do,' Paul said and rummaged it out. The baguette was a soggy pink mess and it was soon all over my gloves, face and clothes, but it was going down. Possibly not my greatest moment of genius, asking Debs to get this from The Picnic Box (a little sandwich shop in Ambleside). But you live and learn.

'Do you want this burger, Sabs?'

'Not really.' I experienced a pang of guilt. Tom didn't want to carry the burger. I hadn't looked, but it was probably oozing mess all over his rucksack.

'You can eat it if you want, Tom.'

I feel guilty about all the food that gets bought or made and carried around various legs and remains uneaten. I don't like wasting anything and vehemently hate wasting food, but while running these challenges it's sometimes hard to eat and you get a bit fussy. Everyone tries very hard to coax me into eating and brings a variety of food to pander to the runner's whims. The whole team knows how important it is to eat regularly.

By the time we reached Great Rigg, the snow had left a decent white dusting on ground that had become a giant Victoria sponge. It was cold but absolutely magical, like being inside a snow globe. Tom knew the route off Fairfield to Hart Crag but was less certain about the best line to Hartsop above How. I wished Dan Duxbury were there. He had shingles. I felt terrible for him; it had affected him hugely and he wasn't running at that time. He had helped me on this section on my second attempt and knew the lines perfectly. I'd loved his boundless energy, his amazing smile and incredibly encouraging words.

Instead Tom was 'winging it' down his chosen line and I was happy to bound along behind him. I knew how to get to the next summit and wasn't particularly bothered if we didn't take the most efficient way to get there, although that sort of thing is especially important to Tom. As things turned out, we progressed well and gained time on the schedule. At Red Screes no one claimed to know the scree run down to Kirkstone, so I was hoping I could remember the turn-off that Dan once showed me. Apart from being a quicker way down, it was a lot more fun. I pushed on ahead and somehow found it, sticking to the grassy edge for the top part but hitting the scree as it became more runnable.

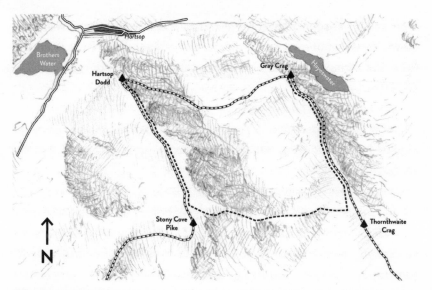

This map shows the two route choices from Hartsop Dodd to Gray Crag. One is direct but drops down an extra 350 metres to climb steeply back up, but the other route results in an extra four-kilometre run along the ridges.

I did stop at my next support point at Kirkstone, but not for long. Jeff Powell Davies and Mike Bottomley took charge of the next leg. Miraculously, it was still daylight when we hit Stony Cove Pike, and with it being so cold, at least it was clear. That meant we had a good line of sight off Hartsop Dodd and could dive off the northern side, taking a shortcut to Gray Crag. It was another sign the round was off to a great start as I easily saved ten minutes that way, but the climb up the other side was brutal and no one was complimenting my route choice. We hit Gray Crag exactly three hours ahead of schedule. Wow! I was so excited I could hardly contain myself and I was still feeling fresh. This was going very well indeed.

I charged along the amazing ridgeline to Yoke; it's all very runnable and my kind of terrain. I hadn't expected any daylight here, let alone the exceptional dusk. It wasn't really dark until we started heading up The Tongue. Jeff found a clever route up to Baystones that I hadn't seen before. It was much faster, and with the ground dry and almost frozen we ended up four hours ahead of schedule.

Jeff and Mike were glad to call it a night at Troutbeck, arriving at 10.06 p.m. instead of 2.12 a.m., which meant they could have a whole night's sleep.

I'm sure the next support team were equally glad to start their short leg a few hours earlier too. It was so cold by then that the ground was definitely freezing hard, but this just meant I could run even faster. Only Johnny Whilock kept up as I navigated my way efficiently from Sour Howes to Sallows to Kentmere, knocking another twenty minutes off the clock.

Just like that, a leg I planned to start in the early morning and continue in daylight became an overnight leg and one of the best nights I had ever had on the fell. There were six of us trotting along the hard, frozen turf in the moonlight. It was so cold the head torch beam kept reflecting off my foggy breath. I was so happy to see Scott Newburn and his mate Andy again. The same pair had waited for me on Kidsty Pike that stormy night on my winter Coast to Coast. They were the reason I had not turned back when Ben asked me to. I convinced him they would be waiting for us on Kidsty as arranged and so we had to press on. And we found them in the violent, ferocious wind ahead of schedule. What a contrast to this night where we were floating along effortlessly through the Far Eastern Fells, ticking off summits. The bog was completely frozen and the air still and cold.

Simon Mills was out in front navigating and I jested with him, shouting 'faster, faster' as I thundered down the descents. I was being childish and reckless and not holding back at all. I felt like it couldn't possibly continue like that. And of course I was right.

I'd never appreciated the Far Eastern Fells as much as I did that night. We were treated to a beautiful pink moon and it was so quiet and still. Most of the time, all we could hear was our own breath and the crunching of frozen snow under our feet. Although there was a small group of us, we were united in our awe of that incredible peace and rarely broke the silence with words. As we approached Mardale Ill Bell, it felt like we were a part of the dawn breaking; and as the light grew stronger, so did our voices.

I'd been running almost continuously for over twenty hours by then, but my legs still felt fresh. I continued to run over High Raise and along the wonderful grassy tracks to Wether Hill. It's easy to navigate this ridge: due north all the way to Arthur's Pike. The sun was starting to glimmer through the cold, misty air and I could see deer grazing on the nearby hills. My schedule had me due in to Martindale at 11.29 a.m. but I scampered in at

5.58 a.m. It had been a very quick first day.

While I had been enjoying a peaceful night on the fells, poor Ben had not had a second's peace in the camper van. My fast running had messed up his plans for a good night's sleep. Instead, when he was rudely wakened by his alarm to check where I was, he saw I was almost at Martindale. He had to get his skates on or else he wasn't going to make it.

In Martindale in the early hours of the morning, the sun was shining but it was so cold my shoelaces were frozen and Ben struggled to undo them. Scott and John were ready and waiting to attack the next leg to Patterdale. It started well, but around Rest Dodd I wasn't feeling right. I can't say quite what was wrong. I was eating well, didn't feel sick and didn't feel sleepy. I just couldn't push up the hills any more. I reasoned that up until this point I had been going inexplicably fast and this might just be the inevitable slowing-down finally hitting. Despite this uneasy feeling, I wasn't going that slowly and was still gaining marginally on my splits. It's just that the gain was less than before.

Analysing the data from my third and fourth rounds, I can see a pattern emerge. The downhill times were pretty similar but the uphill times on the third attempt were clearly slower. There was a reason for this. Somewhere around Martindale, my body fell prey to an old enemy. My asthma was back to haunt me.

At first it was barely noticeable. It wasn't until twenty-four hours later and in increasingly cold conditions that my breathing became noticeably harder, and I can see from my times that this is when I truly started to suffer. For example, on the third attempt I took four hours and twenty-one minutes on the leg between Whitewater Dash and Dodd Wood. On the fourth my time was three hours and forty minutes. And so it continued from Dodd Wood to Binsey, which took two hours and sixteen minutes, almost twenty-five minutes longer than the fourth attempt. I was gasping for breath as I tried to walk up Binsey, feeling awful that I couldn't make conversation with my pacers. I was struggling so hard to breathe that I was having to choose between breathing, talking and eating.

The stretch from Pheasant Inn to Whinlatter was one of my favourite legs and this third attempt was once again special. I had the magic trio of Dazmo,

Rick and Matt B., who had supported me on the Pennine Way FKT. The weather was great, albeit cold, but my breathing was poor. Darren could see I was suffering and stuck by my side feeding me Mountain Fuel jellies and water while the other two concentrated on where we were going.

If I was getting frustrated with my breathing and lack of ability to push up the hills, then I tried to make up for it by charging down the hills, something that required a lot less energy. Miraculously, I was still holding my splits. I wasn't sure how, because by now everyone around me could hear the problem as my wheezy breathing broke the evening quiet. I was starting to cough too and no amount of inhaler doses were helping to settle me.

I reached Whinlatter at 11.07 p.m. on Sunday, my third day running. It was dark, cold and starting to spit. I had a short sleep there before heading up Grisedale Pike, but despite two hours of rest I took over an hour to ascend Grisedale due to the deterioration in my breathing (ten minutes longer than I needed on my successful round when I hadn't taken a rest). The impact of my asthma is shown in the splits for the downhill sections, which are remarkably similar.

The real deterioration came on the next leg from Rannerdale to Newlands, when I experienced respiratory failure. On both attempts in 2021 the weather was similar, the day starting out calm and dry but quickly deteriorating into a wet, windy and wild day. The time difference on this leg, though, was seven hours versus five: a two-hour difference. Those sorts of losses weren't sustainable. I remember reaching the bottom of Ard Crags and having to stop and lean on my poles as I gasped for air, trying to loosen the clothing around my throat because I felt I was being strangled. I had an audible wheeze and also some pops and crackles indicating I had fluid on my lungs. My lips were cyanotic; my respiratory system was severely compromised. That was the moment I decided I would have to abandon the attempt but, being close to the next support point, I pressed on.

At Newlands Hause we were all soaked to the skin and freezing. The rain was turning rapidly to sleet but Ben briefed us that the incoming front was expected to bring a worsening of the weather, with the potential for snow. I clambered into the van. I didn't really care about the forecast. There was a much bigger problem as far as I was concerned: oxygen and the lack of it. I told Ben I would sleep there for six hours. I was still well ahead of schedule and if I was to have any chance of getting back out again I had to control my breathing. To do that, I needed warm air and rest. I changed out of my sodden clothes, crawled into the camper van bed and took a puff on my inhaler, tipping me into a fit of spluttering coughs. I tried to sleep but it took a while. My breathing was so rapid I couldn't count my breaths per minute. Sucking on my inhaler just made me cough. I felt I was being strangled, even as I drifted off.

Less than two hours later, I was on Robinson in the worst weather you could imagine for May. What had happened to my six-hour sleep? There was snow on the ground and snow in the air, a blizzard so bad we couldn't see where we were going and a wind so biting it ripped through our clothing like it wasn't there. I was screaming at Martin Stone.

'Martin, I'm going to hold on to Mingma now. I'm doing it for safety reasons. I want to get off this fucking hill.'

Oh my god, I thought, *he can't hear me. Or he doesn't care. Why is he wearing Y-fronts on his head? He doesn't even look cold. He looks like a child who's seen snow for the first time.*

'Martin! I want … ' Fuck's sake. 'Martin!! MARTIN!!!' Was I just talking to myself? Could anyone hear me? Had I died already? I couldn't breathe. I was passing out. Thank fuck for Mingma Sherpa. He seemed to be the only one who gave a shit if I lived or died.

'Martin,' I whispered when Mingma got his attention. I literally couldn't get the breath out to be heard. I was gasping so much he had to come closer to hear. 'I am not proud of what we're doing. This is a mountain rescue situation. We need to go down.'

'We are your mountain rescue, Sabs. You're fine!'

'I'm not fine. We need to go down.'

I wasn't really sure whether I was saying anything, whether anyone could hear me. Why no one was listening. Why everyone was ignoring the obvious.

'IT IS OVER.'

Everything went black. Then it was all white. Then it flicked between the two: black, white, black, white. It was like when my eyelids close from sleep deprivation and my brain is too slow to notice. Except I kept going floppy and collapsing in the snow. Was I losing consciousness or was I falling over in that sleety, snowy, slippery mess of a downhill? I didn't know and I didn't care. I'd given up. I might just die there on that mountain because some moronic men thought I should keep going. Or maybe they were deaf. Or maybe I wasn't actually speaking?

Why was I doing this? It was crazy! I should have stayed in the camper van until my breathing was better. Instead I'd been woken after an hour instead of six and told I had to go then or I wasn't going to get the record.

I didn't want the record. I wanted to breathe.

'Mingma, we need to go down.'

'We are going down.'

Oh, thank goodness. As we started downhill, my lungs no longer had to make such an effort. I was basically falling with gravity and I was so tired I didn't even try to brace myself, so it was just an effortless slide down the snow. As we got lower, the air got warmer and the wind less violent. I was just so relieved we'd all made it down safe and sound. We had sent Jacob Tonkin back to Newlands when we were halfway up Robinson because he was hypothermic, and poor Steve was getting so cold he'd resorted to doing sprint reps out and back to stop himself from freezing. I'd asked Tim Miller to accompany Jacob back down to the support van and I'd felt bad because Tim had come all the way out to Robinson to run with me. But he's such a good egg he didn't mind at all. Ironically, the next time I met him I was out supporting John Kelly on his bid to break my record. Tim had just popped out over the brow as we started to ascend to Slight Side from Illgill Head. Once again I had to ask him to run off to the rescue to grab the support bag off Phil, who had been struggling to keep up in the heat. Once again he didn't hesitate. It's incredible how wonderful fell runners are, willing to go to whatever lengths are required to help.

Pacers take their job seriously. While they enjoy coming out for a run in good company, they are always aware of the task at hand and their role in the mission. I'm the same when I go out to support someone. You forget about what you would like to be doing and concentrate on how you can best help the person taking on the challenge. I helped John Knapp on his Bob Graham attempt; he chose to set off in less than ideal conditions and he wanted me to do the first leg for him. It's not my favourite and it also meant running in the dark, but I wanted to do whatever was most helpful. I remember I had to work so hard to try and keep up with John on the ascents. His legs were fresh and he's a strong climber and in addition I had to carry the bag of kit and help with navigation. Luckily, I could get some reprieve to catch my breath on the descents. I threw myself at the task and did whatever I could to be helpful. John had helped me on various Wainwrights attempts but it wasn't just a quid pro quo. I also wanted to be a part of John's adventure. I wanted to be a part of the team that would help John succeed.

So there I was on Robinson in appalling weather, relying on my champions – Steve, Martin and Mingma – accompanying me on my ridiculous challenge, asking for nothing in return and wishing only to help me as best they could to reach my goal. So they didn't want me to give up, they wanted me to press on despite the horrible conditions. However, I had already pushed myself beyond simple discomfort. The last three days had been punishing on my lungs. The cold air had done a number of things: bronchoconstriction leading to pulmonary oedema; wheezing from air that could not escape my passages; and my poor airway lining so irritated I was constantly coughing. My chest was so tight it felt like someone was trying to strangle me.

Looking back, if I had completed this round I could never have claimed a record, given the state I was in. Even if I wasn't physically assisted I was utterly dependent on my support team. If they hadn't been there, I wouldn't have known the right direction to go in or been able to look after myself. I was in no fit state to 'compete'. I didn't even remember reaching the summits of Hindscarth or Dale Head. For all I knew we missed them out, and that wasn't acceptable to me. It's not worth risking your life for a record and I am ashamed that I tried to continue given my condition.

I never understood why John Kelly finished that attempt on the Pennine Way with a bleeding gastric ulcer: a life-threatening condition. Or why

Damian Hall had staggered over the Coast to Coast finish line for a marginal FKT despite suffering from hyponatraemia, low levels of sodium in the blood that can also be life-threatening. Or why I had staggered up the steps of Moot Hall like Mr Blobby at the end of my second attempt. After my third attempt, I decided to impose more criteria on myself: no ibuprofen and finishing the round in a state I would be proud of, not like a criminal, not broken, not like a Smurf who'd smoked too many fags, but as a true athlete.

Yet still I carried on. After a short sleep in Portinscale to warm up and after some hot food, I was once again sent on my not-so-merry way. The problem was that once I climbed into the warm van and rested, my breathing improved and I felt better. Able to move again, once I got back into the cold air my lungs were quickly distressed. This next leg was much lower, starting with a long road walk to Latrigg, and should have been more tolerable. The weather was tamer, still cold and wet but not the ferocious blizzard we'd endured on the ridge. But the problem wasn't the weather; the problem was that I still couldn't breathe. The grey gloom of evening soon turned to night as Paul Nelson, Steve B. and I climbed to Walla Crag and then Bleaberry Fell. It was painfully slow and depressing. Then we hit the heathery, boggy heights of Ashness Fell. This was already my least favourite leg, and in the wet and wild wind, it prompted me finally to make the right decision and sack it off.

In adventure racing we always say that you should never make a decision to quit before having a good sleep. Sometimes sleep deprivation can make things seem worse than they are. With this in the back of my mind, and having come so far along the route, I suggested we push on to Armboth but then drop to Thirlmere. I thought that once there we would all be able to get in the camper van, have a kip and then reassess. That way, if I changed my mind after resting, I could head back out. It was so hard to let go of my dream.

While we had signal we hit the emergency button on the tracker to alert the team to what was happening and Steve tried to call Ben before we descended out of range. Unfortunately, we were unable to make contact with anyone. Down at Thirlmere there was no camper van, no car and no support crew. It was about 5 a.m. and dark, cold and wet. We all clambered into Steve's four-person bothy. Despite the noise of the wind billowing the bag, you could still hear my wheezing at about ninety breaths a minute. Even at rest, I was now severely compromised.

We waited and waited, cold and unable to sleep on the hard wet ground, unable to get comfortable and with me unable to slow my breathing. At some point Steve offered to run the ten kilometres to his car. That would take time but it seemed our only option. Paul and I waited, freezing and knackered. The bothy was no longer keeping us even vaguely warm, so we headed for Armboth's public toilets. Eventually, Steve came back and rescued us and he took us to Borrowdale, where the rest of the team were waiting with no signal and no tracking information. We updated them on the situation and I told them I was not continuing.

TEN

BREATHE EASY

For five days after I abandoned the third attempt, I struggled with severe asthma. It was so bad on the first night that, despite being utterly exhausted, I couldn't sleep. My respiratory rate was too fast, my breathing was noisy and I was coughing a lot. I didn't dwell on the failure of the round but focused instead on regaining my health. Strangely, my legs felt fine. I certainly wasn't hobbling around like I was after the Spine or my second Wainwrights attempt. In fact, if it hadn't been for the inability to breathe, I would probably have gone straight back out on the fells for a run. After a course of steroids, my breathing improved and I started to think about running again.

Then I was hit with another blow: a tooth abscess. I'd had these before, but this one was different and much more painful. I went to the dentist and had the tooth removed, but instead of easing, the pain got dramatically worse. I struggled for three days, in so much pain I couldn't think straight. Despite taking all the painkillers permitted, the pain was not subsiding. Finally, I went back to the dentist, who explained I had a dry socket. If you've never had one of these, trust me, you don't want one. The clot that should be protecting the extraction site had been dislodged, exposing nerves and bone to bacteria and contact with food. The result is an immense amount of pain. I needed several trips to the dentist, another course of antibiotics and lots more painkillers.

In amongst the pain and trips to the dentist, I somehow managed to support a leg for John Kelly on his Pennine Way FKT. I was surprised my legs could function two weeks after the third attempt, but I was in too much pain to consider planning another attempt.

Despite this, the following week – only three weeks after the attempt – I was out running again and even getting some personal bests on Strava. *How bizarre*, I thought. *I wonder if I could have another go at the Wainwrights this year?* Then I shut the thought down, thinking of my spreadsheet and of having to ask Ben for support and then contacting my long-suffering support team once again to ask for help. And who would want to help this three-time failure? Surely they would all think it a lost cause?

I learnt a lot from my third attempt about how badly my lungs could be affected by cold weather. I also felt remorseful for not having addressed the issue sooner. It wasn't the first time I'd suffered from this problem. I'd experienced something similar climbing to Everest Base Camp, on the Spine Race in January 2020 and on my Coast to Coast run in December 2020. So on three occasions I'd experienced breathing issues associated with prolonged periods of inhaling cold air, and yet I hadn't taken the time to do anything about it. On all three occasions the asthma had left me severely debilitated, but because I'd pressed on and finished the races I hadn't felt the need to deal with it. In retrospect, though, I could see there had been a worsening of the symptoms. So after the third attempt I spent time talking to doctors about the problem, although to be honest I am still none the wiser and have no concrete way to resolve it. My only conclusion was that if I was going to do another Wainwrights attempt, it might be best if it were warmer.

What else could I improve on to ensure a successful outcome? There were plenty of lessons from the second attempt. One of my key concerns was fluid retention; how on earth did I manage to look full-term pregnant with triplets? I did plenty of research and found a lot of interesting scientific literature. In one experiment, prisoners were fed fifty per cent of their normal caloric intake and then weighed regularly. When the men were fed properly, they lost weight, due to fluid loss. It seems that when the body is in a stressed state with lots of cortisol floating around, it retains water to hold on to every precious drop of fluid. Dehydration causes a similar phenomenon. So stress (from exercise, fatigue, calorie and water deprivation) can cause raised cortisol levels and water retention. Inflammation also causes swelling and fluid accumulation at the site of an injury. This is why my right leg was more swollen than my left. It's likely the inflammation was largely responsible for exacerbating all the fluid retention I suffered on the second attempt.

Aside from the injury and the waterlogged ground conditions that were perhaps beyond my control, I felt I could also improve on my sleep strategy. The main strategy of the second attempt had been to find the limit, or at least *my* limit for how little I could sleep and still be functional. I had definitely pushed it too far. Partly this was a consequence of Covid-19 and not being allowed to 'sleep out'. So I was limited in where I could rest. Having started at Moot Hall, my first planned sleep for the first and second attempts had been at my house in Langdale. Yet this meant going without sleep for just over forty-eight hours, which was a little too much.

Looking back, it would have been more productive to sleep at Tilberthwaite, the support point before Langdale. This would have meant stopping to sleep at 11.37 p.m. instead of 3.46 a.m. Thanks to sleep deprivation, that leg from Tilberthwaite to Langdale took about an hour longer than it should have done, with me falling asleep on my feet and staggering around instead of running or at least marching up the hills. So for the third attempt I changed my plan to ensure I slept in the earlier part of the night, between 11 p.m. and 1 a.m. where possible. This was a better strategy because it meant if I was significantly ahead of time and arrived in daylight, I could afford to postpone the sleep to the next support point and still sleep during the dark hours.

I also didn't want to risk injuring myself in the way I had done on the second attempt. In particular, I was keen to avoid the long traverse across the slope of The Nab. So I went back to the maps and reverted to the original route Steve did, but instead of cutting through the non-open-access land from Beda Head to The Nab, I made a slightly longer detour to go around the end of the wall at Bannerdale Beck. I also thought about the strategy that Paul had used to keep his muscles in as good a state as possible. He had relied on a whole team of masseurs and physiotherapists to help him. While I didn't have access to that scale of expertise, I did have friends who might be able to help by just rubbing my legs a bit to disperse the retained fluid at each support point.

I didn't see myself in contention for taking anyone's record. Even now, people congratulate me for taking the record, but I hate that phrase. You can't take a record from someone; you can only make a new one. I haven't taken anything; I have completed my challenge successfully, running all the Wainwrights in under six days. No one will ever take that away from me. That's why I can give my devoted support to help the next fell runner 'take the record'. A friend told me I was inhuman for not feeling anything but joy for Anna Troup when she set a new female FKT for the Pennine Way. I have no motivation to go back out there and try to beat her time. I'm not saying I'll never do the Pennine Way again. I still want to beat my own target of seventy-two hours and would also prefer to do it south to north next time. There are women who can beat the current men's record of fifty-eight hours and four minutes. But my goal will remain under seventy-two hours: realistic but challenging.

Of course, the greater the challenge, the sweeter the reward, but also the greater the risk of failure. And fear of failure is the greatest barrier to success. Paul Tierney achieved an incredible feat setting a new record, and he didn't need a second or third or even fourth attempt. Yet there is a part of me that wonders whether Paul regrets not having set his sights higher. Paul played the safer game of only aiming to beat Steve's time. I aimed much higher to break that six-day barrier: a real challenge must have a risk of failure. Of course any current record can be broken; the question is, who is not too afraid to try? But even if you do fail, trust me, in the wise words of my husband Ben: 'No one cares.' No one laughs at you, no one is nasty, most people empathise, so get up and give it another go. Why try four times? Why not? I had nothing to lose and everything to gain.

Tenacious little fucker.

Even so, I told myself, this must really be the last try. I had to do it this time. On the first three attempts, I had set off confident that I could do it. Each time I had failed. Covid-19 had stopped me. Injury had stopped me. And finally, only six weeks earlier, unseasonably cold weather had triggered my asthma and that had stopped me. I was more determined than ever to finally put this obsession to bed.

My mission was to run around the Wainwright summits as quickly as possible with the following rules: to visit the summits as described by Wainwright; to do this in a continuous round, which for me meant not leaving the route as others have done to be driven back to a house or hotel for a kip; to navigate myself round my chosen route, respecting access law and the Countryside Code; to finish in good health and a respectable state and avoid taking any painkillers as far as possible, particularly anti-inflammatories; to enjoy the round with friends and not put anyone at undue risk; and to complete the round in under six days.

During the years of preparation and previous attempts, I had spent hours staring at my spreadsheet of Wainwrights logistics. It detailed all the summits, the approximate time it would take me to run between those summits, the cumulative time spent running, the date and time of arrival at each summit, the name of pacers accompanying me on particular legs and the road support at each support point. (I would not have been able to go as fast as I did without the vast numbers of people who came out to support me, over fifty in total.) So the spreadsheet was huge. It was tiring just scrolling through it, let alone running to each of those summits.

Preparing for the Wainwrights was a massive undertaking in itself. I prepared kit boxes. I made sure I had at least two sets of everything I expected to have with me on each leg. That way, one set could be in the van ready for the next leg while the other set was with me on the current leg. I had recced every section at least twice and the trickier bits as many as five times so I knew the best way to go. I had prepared laminated sections of each leg for the pacers: a 1:25,000 OS map with the route marked and, on the back, the summits relevant for that section and the ETA for each summit.

I prepared my food as much as I could, buying various ready meals, quiches and pizzas that Ben could quickly heat up for me at support points. I put together a box of sports nutrition filled with my regular, tried and tested brands: Mountain Fuel jellies, sachets of Mountain Fuel recovery drink to mix with fresh milk into shakes and some Chia Charge bars that are a bit like flapjacks. As much as I can feel the benefit of using properly formulated nutrition, there isn't anything quite as nourishing or encouraging as homemade cakes. Hence, I also bought twelve boxes of tray bakes and cakes (twenty slices in each) from Ginger Bakers of Kendal for my supporters and me to enjoy on the way round (have I mentioned I like cake?).

My hill kit included lightweight waterproof jackets and PrimaLoft jackets, hats and gloves, with multiple options appropriate for different weather conditions, trekking poles and pole gloves, buffs, a large plastic kit box with wet and cold weather gear (more gloves and waterproof mitts, heavier waterproofs, more PrimaLoft), additional kit I could change into if my clothes got wet. I also had eight pairs of La Sportiva Mutants, some in size 40.5 and some in size 41 for when my feet were getting a bit fat. My first aid kit included my all-important inhaler, Imodium, paracetamol, blister plasters, foot tape, lip salve, mini toothbrush and toothpaste, toilet paper and a bag to put used toilet paper in (nice).

I spent a lot of time organising as much as I could to alleviate pressure on the support team. In that regard, the third attempt had been a useful rehearsal. I had made a thorough schedule for it, but after months of training I was faster and knew the route better than I imagined. As a consequence, I got too far ahead: eleven hours at one point. This caused Ben a lot of grief. He had to make sure all the pacers were aware of what was going on, as their anticipated start times were changing so drastically. Support teams will factor in being two hours up or down on a schedule, but not eleven hours. That gap also changed some day sections into night sections and vice versa, which impacted my planned sleep locations. On the fourth attempt, I had my actual times from the third attempt to rely on rather than my earlier estimated times, at least as far as Whinlatter, after which I would be running faster. From that point on the third attempt I had been incapacitated by asthma and snow on the leg between Newlands and Portinscale that had made conditions slow going.

Having a more accurate schedule contributed a lot to the success of the fourth attempt. Although I still managed to get a bit ahead of my timings, I was always within an hour or two: much more manageable. I ate more sensibly as well: proper hot food in the support van and more digestible carbohydrates on the hill. A lot of my calories came from Mountain Fuel jellies, which gave me an instant energy boost and were easy to ingest. The weather wasn't perfect but it was okay. And, unlike the second attempt, I got the amount of sleep exactly right. I hardly ever needed a quick kip on the fell: just once, in fact, and only for around five minutes – or at least, that's what I remember. Other than that, I was quite awake and only flagged at the very end on the Duddon End to Tilberthwaite leg.

Friday 11 June. 7.03 a.m. I set off from my home in Great Langdale with Giles Ruck, Darren Moore and my husband Ben. It felt very low key and a bit déjà vu. I wasn't as excited as I was six weeks ago. There was frustration inside of me, knowing that I should have done this already. I had to do it this time. Yet there was a nagging fear that everything had already gone wrong. I hadn't slept well the previous night. I'd woken with a dodgy tummy and I knew Ben had one too. It must have been the Thai curry we'd had for dinner. I was really stiff and sore and didn't feel like moving at all, let alone running. But I had to hide that and pretend that I was fighting fit and raring to go because Ben had told me categorically that this was the last time he was willing to support me. Quite frankly, I was fed up of the whole thing myself. So I told myself to keep calm and carry on because you never know what will happen.

It wasn't the nicest morning: drizzly, grey and windy, but the forecast suggested it would improve later. I was holding back my pace and taking it steady as I knew I hadn't got the speed in my pacers that I needed to go full pelt like I had last time with John Kelly. Conditions were slippery and a bit wilder than expected, so it was just as well. Even so, coming into Rydal, I was pleasantly surprised to find I was only a few minutes behind the third attempt time, given that I had put in about ten per cent less effort. I knew this leg so well that every step was in the right direction and I wasn't hanging around.

I did stop in at the Badger Bar on this round, having been told off the last time for running straight on and skipping the support. I needed to check on my little furry patient Blea, one of my friend Debs's three collies. Since I first met Debs in 2019, she had supported me on my Pennine Way and Coast to Coast FKTs in her little camper van. She had recently moved up to the Lake District and we'd become great friends. We often go for walks and runs with her collies Phroaig, Swift and Blea and I sometimes run with her husband Scott too.

So when Debs called me the night before the fourth attempt, worrying about Blea, naturally I wanted to make sure she was okay. At 9 p.m. she brought Blea over to my house so I could examine a random swelling on her jaw. I had known on the phone it was nothing urgent but I knew also that Debs would worry herself silly all night. The lump was soft and felt full of fluid, so I found a needle and syringe in the house and drained it. It was just a cyst and I explained to Debs it might refill a little but was nothing to worry about. I also promised to check her again at Rydal on my way through next day. So there I was on my record-breaking round checking Blea's mysterious mass.

'It's all good, Debs.'

Ben and Giles were glad they had made it, but poor Alastair Black would be my only supporter on leg two. I first met Al when Ben and I went out to support Gwyn Stokes on a Bob Graham Round. Al was managing his road support and we paced a leg. I didn't hesitate to ask him to help me on my round; I knew he was really good at supporting, made yummy cakes and was great company. I knew also that supporting this whole leg on his own would be tough for him, but I was prepared to take it easy and I knew the navigation, which lightened the burden. We had a great time and this next section went well, taking about the same time as the third attempt.

I even managed to find the scree run off Red Screes down to the Kirkstone car park, a good effort given I had only ever been down there twice before, and worth it because it saves a lot of time. A wave of nausea came over me as I got into the van. I felt too sick to eat anything, but Ben was insisting and more or less force-feeding me. He might have regretted that when I asked him to pass me a bucket and I brought it all back up. Oh dear.

Was it all going wrong? I never vomit. I looked in the bucket. There seemed to be weird black bits.

'Ben, what are those?'

'Grapes, I think.' Weird. I ate those a few days ago. They must have been sat in my stomach for ages. Perhaps it wasn't the curry after all?

'I feel better now.' And I did feel better. In fact, I felt great.

Tom Hare turned up in the nick of time to join Paul Wilson for the third leg. Things were starting to feel good. I managed to eat a little on the way up to Stony Cove and as I reached the flatter, grassy track I lengthened my stride on the way to Hartsop Dodd. It was still daylight and dry so it was a no-brainer to take the shortcut to Gray Crag. That saved me retracing my steps back to Caudale Moor and going round the horseshoe but there's a bit more to climb and I have to say it's a pig of an ascent back up after crossing the beck. Overall, it saved me about ten minutes. Now we were really shifting, ticking off the summits in pleasant evening conditions as we reached Troutbeck and then Kentmere in good time.

I was going well, but that was a challenge for my pacers. The late decision to start meant I didn't have a huge pool of people free and willing to support me, especially as races were starting to happen again. So I was so lucky that my running club Lonsdale were able to chip in. On this leg I had Joe Hobbs from the club, Fi Marley Patterson (from ITV news), who I met supporting a Bob Graham, and Rich White, a friend of mine who had also supported me on the Pennine Way FKT. It's a bit of a slog up Shipman Knotts and too steep to run, but after the climb it's a lovely, grassy and runnable route to Kentmere Pike. If it's not too boggy it's a good trot off the trails and on open fell down to Garburn Pass. The ground wasn't frozen like last time so it was a little boggier and definitely slower across the Far Eastern Fells – Tarn Crag, Grey Crag, Selside Pike and Branstree – before heading to Gatescarth and rockier going.

It was already a stunning night when we said goodbye to Rich before Harter Fell. He turned to run home and the three of us who remained trotted along High Street, one of my favourite sections. Dawn revealed deer scattering across the landscape as we ran into Martindale. The sun was already shining as I strolled up Hallin Fell with some fresh pacers;

it promised to be a beautiful day. I was hoping I could remember the good trods that Scott Newburn had shown me last time out and that the bracken wouldn't be too high for me to plunge off the side of Place Fell for the direct route into Patterdale. It all went to plan and you could feel the excitement brewing in the team as I arrived.

Matt Beresford, Darren Moore and Rachel were ready and waiting to take me onwards to Helvellyn. I met Matt through Darren; he's another humble, local fell runner and now another good running friend. They had brought Rachel along and it was so nice to meet another female runner. I learnt she was getting ready for a Bob Graham attempt later in the year. Darren was his usual encouraging self, excited to let me know about every top we hit better than last time. It wasn't surprising I was doing better. This was where my asthma had started to slow me down. Whizzing along Catstye Cam ridge, we were soon bounding off the edge of Birkhouse Moor, another deviation from Steve Birkinshaw's route. I much prefer this grassy direct descent to Glenridding over the rocky footpath to Gillside.

Claire Nance and Phil Withnall, a couple from Lonsdale Fell Runners, joined me on this next leg. It was so nice to see them and have their company. I had actually met Claire a decade before at Cambridge, so it was a wonderful surprise to discover she had moved up to Lancaster. Both are handy runners. I had raced with Phil in The Fellsman in April 2019. We came sixth and seventh two minutes apart, so were well matched on pace. Claire is quicker than me but not into such long distances, although she has done a brilliant Ramsay Round. But it was now getting a bit hot so I decided to back off the pace. I knew it would be cooler once we were up high and it made sense to take it easy on the slog up. Despite my caution, I was sick again when I put a gel in too quickly, although I felt better again afterwards. Having run through a whole night with no sleep and done more than thirty hours of running, I expected to be feeling it.

Once up high, there was a gentle breeze and a good temperature. My energy levels were waxing and waning a little but Claire and Phil kept me right with good chat, food and fluids. I was determined to come off Clough Head and hit the Coach Road with more energy than last time, but I still wasn't able to run much of the tarmacked trail. It should have been easy, but my legs were heavy. Still, I made it to Dockray in good time and was definitely gaining on my third attempt. I also didn't need to stop for a sleep there as I had last time. So I cracked on with my new pacers, Paul Nelson and Andy Jackson.

When I hit Troutbeck on the A66 I was ready for my first scheduled sleep. I had been going for about forty hours without a rest. I asked Ben to wake me up after an hour and a half and I fell asleep easily. I was excited to wake up to find Peter Sowerby and Steve Birkinshaw waiting for me. Phil again joined me for a third and final leg in support. I reminded myself to relax: Peter had told me when he met me here on the third attempt I had scared him. He said he'd never seen me so focused. I think it was my fierce determination; it had made him petrified of making a mistake on the navigation. But this time he knew the way as well as I did.

It was great to see Steve again. Both Peter and I were bewildered at the way he navigated up Souther Fell, bashing through bracken up the steep wet slope without the use of a GPS device, watch, compass or map, relying instead on some sixth sense. We were less enamoured with Mungrisdale Common and the long slog to get to a rather disappointing pile of stones. On the way, all three of us had managed to fall into the same bog and we were all plastered in mud, but at least that made us chuckle. And that was the last hard bit on this leg. From there, I could pick up speed and motor along to Mosedale. We were clearly gaining time because when we got there Ben wasn't ready for us and the next leg's pacers had not yet arrived.

'Anyone fancy another leg?' I asked hopefully, after eating something. Phil was shattered. He'd already done three legs for me in twenty-four hours and deserved a rest. Pete was knackered as the pace was too sharp for him. That left Stevie B. He agreed to start on the leg until the others caught us up, but in the end I decided to have a ten-minute kip to give the others a chance to arrive, which they promptly did.

It's always hard graft up to Carrock Fell, a steep, semi-grassy, semi-rubbly wet slog. I remembered climbing it with Jeff Powell Davies and Howard Dracup on the second attempt in the last of the evening sun, a total contrast to this mizzle. Still Mingma Sherpa, Paul Cornforth, Lou Osborn and I were in good spirits. Mingma was quite focused, having taken on the role of navigator, although I remember at one point he was running backwards down a hill filming us faster than we were running forwards. That's some talent. I hadn't expected to gain time on this leg but I did. The ground conditions were muddier and slower than before, so the time gain could only be a consequence of my improved lung function.

Debs met us at Whitewater Dash and I checked Blea again; the lump was still there but much smaller, so things were improving. Then I continued to the Skiddaw leg with her husband Scott and Mingma. It was fairly straightforward until we got to Ullock Pike: I hate the descent of this stupid ridge. You can bracken-bash your way off the side for the shortest line. Or double back along the ridge and descend off Carl Side down the tourist route. Or something in between, with the problem that replicating 'in between' is difficult. You do something slightly different and these minor variations inevitably feel slower. All the options are rough and all are painful on tired, aching legs. At least once safely down, the leg was pretty much done. A short climb to Dodd and then a swooping forest track down to the car park for everyone's favourite next leg: Binsey.

Only John Knapp could face the tedium of this section. I didn't dare ask how many times he'd done it before. John's an avid FKT supporter, always willing to help, but sadly his knees don't allow him to do the more gnarly stuff, so Binsey suits him. The road run definitely felt better than last time. I didn't feel like I was being strangled as we climbed the hill and was delighted to see two young children on the fell also ticking off their Wainwrights. They really picked me up, giving me chocolates as we climbed the hill.

I had a big support team at Pheasant Inn: the dynamic duo of Darren and Rich with Andy Jackson and Paul Nelson, who had completed the Petite Trotte à Léon together, although at 300 kilometres there's nothing 'little' about that trot. Darren and Rich had done this Wainwrights leg with me six weeks earlier, so we all knew exactly what we were doing. Except when it started raining, we realised I didn't have a waterproof jacket. How did that happen? Luckily, it was towards the end of the leg and Andy happily lent me his, knowing he'd be getting into a warm car while I carried on.

I arrived early into Whinlatter at 9.24 p.m. and it was still light. I wasn't supposed to be there, according to my schedule, until 1.31 a.m. We decided to move my next planned sleep stop to Rannerdale, where it would be dark. I felt good and was happy to see Mike Bottomley. It felt like we picked up the pace and the next leg was certainly faster than on the third attempt, despite the claggy darkness. The climb up to Grisedale was easier compared to last time, when I was struggling to breathe, but in the murk it wasn't easy to keep the best line along the ridge. I messed up the descent off Whiteside slightly, but we had made up so much time it didn't matter.

At Rannerdale I discussed with Ben how long I should sleep. He wanted me to have two hours and I only wanted an hour and a half, so we compromised on an hour and forty-five minutes. Then I woke up after an hour and a half and decided I wanted to go. Ben was also sleep-deprived and grumpy that I had woken him up. He told me he didn't have time to make me breakfast but I didn't care; I found some things to eat that didn't need cooking and told Mike we would head off soon. My pacers for the next leg, Phil and Jackie Scarf, had not yet arrived but I knew they would catch us. I know Jackie and Phil from adventure racing. They're great friends and I love that they are now retired and can spend so much time having adventures together and with their children.

Jackie and Phil caught us earlier than I expected, before we'd even summited Rannerdale Knotts, the first summit of the leg. It was still dark and I knew I was ahead of the third attempt because then I'd been treated to the most stunning sunrise. This time, the conditions were benign but a little damp later on. I still felt spritely, was eating and drinking and didn't feel weary. I think the sleep had done me good.

By now I was well over halfway round, but the tale was far from written. I still hadn't passed Armboth, where the third attempt had ended. Trotting down from Scar Crags col to the stream before the slog up Ard Crags, I recalled how on the third attempt I had been gasping for air at this point. At Ard Crags, I'd take a couple of steps up the steep, grassy climb and then stop to hang on my poles and catch my breath, taking pointless puffs of Ventolin which never reached my lungs because I was coughing so much. This time was different. Although it still felt hard to plug up the steep, grassy mound, I summited quickly and capably. Feeling jubilant, I trotted along the ridge to Knott Rigg, the final summit on this leg, and was still able to run the grassy descent into Newlands Hause.

I was excited to see my La Sportiva teammate Jacob Snochowski, who was joining us on the next leg. Jacob is one of those rare people who is caring, quietly confident and content with his lot, which makes him an amazing person to be around. It's not a surprise that his first career was in nursing and I imagine he was one of the best. But I can see him being even happier sitting in his railway signal box at Foxfield admiring the beautiful Lakeland scenery. Despite these traits, he's an extremely competitive and talented ultrarunner. When I arrived and saw some kind of supportive contraption strapped to his ankle, I felt a pang of guilt. Surely he shouldn't be out on the hill? But Jacob wouldn't have missed it for the world. He was there to make a difference and help me succeed this final time. He was prepared to set aside all his running hopes for the moment just to make sure I could succeed at mine.

Phil and Jackie were more relaxed at this point. Initially they had both been a little uncertain whether they could keep up and manage two legs. After they'd settled into that familiar adventure-racing pace, we all just cruised up Robinson. Phil's knee is not in the best shape but he knows the hills and will cut corners here and there so he can still join in. The sun was shining, a stark contrast to six weeks earlier when I was in a blizzard, sliding on wet, sludgy snow, gasping and wondering if I was going to expire. At Cat Bells I became nostalgic, remembering the bagpipes my friend Johnny was playing as I summited the last summit on my second attempt. I had thrown my arms up with my poles in the air, elated that I had bagged all the summits in one round for the first time in my life – even while knowing it would not be the last.

Descending Cat Bells, my legs felt good. Keswick was a landmark: almost two-thirds round with two really tough legs and two only slightly less tough legs before the home stretch. I always manage to turn things into a positive, so while I still had the hardest terrain ahead of me, feeling in great shape meant I was ready to tackle it. I was desperate to get to Armboth to put the misery of the third attempt behind me, and that would come on the next leg.

Coming into Keswick, I felt lifted by so many folk turning out. In Portinscale someone even cheered me from a back garden. As I turned up the street to Moot Hall, there were more cheers as I bounded up the steps. There were lots of friends there, including Andy Slattery, the assistant chief constable of Cumbria who had the heartrending job of pulling the plug on my first attempt. Somehow it seemed appropriate that Andy should join me on this successful attempt and it was an opportunity to get to know him better. So on I pressed from the Moot Hall (the place where Steve, Paul and I had started previous Wainwrights attempts) to complete the loop that I had started from my home in Great Langdale this time.

Sadly, Andy only got to know 'whiney' Sabs. Shortly after leaving Keswick and the excitement of seeing all my friends, and after bagging the easy summit of Latrigg, the penny dropped that I was now on the 'shit' leg. And I was starting to feel it. So it was good that Tory Miller was with us. Tory deserves an entire chapter devoted to her adorable soul. She helped Paul Tierney on his record-breaking round and was probably at every support point too, while also working quietly in the background to get various pieces of much needed kit here, there and everywhere. When she got wind of my 2020 attempts, she wanted in. She wanted to do as much of my support as she could. She even told me she would book time off work to do what I needed. I felt a little overwhelmed by the enthusiasm. Surely I wasn't that important? But, knowing I would need all the help I could get, I was delighted to have her support on the second attempt. My fondest memory was reaching the summit of The Nab to see Tory's beaming grin as she handed me some hot chips, a cup of tea and some cake.

Tory had been back to South Africa to see her family and got caught up in the Covid-19 mayhem. When she tried to get home, a new South African variant was raging and then she caught Covid herself. I couldn't quite understand why she was so desperate to get back to cold, wet England, but her home was now here and she clearly wanted to help me with my next Wainwrights attempt. She had booked a flight back in April but kept testing positive, so remained stuck and was gutted to miss the third attempt. I jested I would have to do it again so she could be involved.

So now here she was, with me on the 'shit' leg, being her lovely, jolly self and taking my mind off my aching body. She had joined me earlier on this round on the Skiddaw leg, when I complained that every water bottle she gave me tasted of bleach, pepper or Mountain Fuel. I had been such a diva. It was a wonder Miss Grumpy Pants had any friends at all, let alone this lovely person who wanted to come out again. So instead of moaning at Tory, I just ranted about the shitfest beneath my feet: the bogginess, the heathery tussocks and their absolute indecency in making me lift my weary legs or else tripping me when I didn't. Raven Crag, while an absolute pain in the arse out and back, does at least reward you with a serene view over Thirlmere. Then the proper boggy, tussocky slog really began, but at least I was only two kilometres and one summit away from Armboth.

Waiting for me at Armboth was Steve Ashworth, who had been hired before the third attempt to make a film for my sponsors. Steve had been delighted I failed, since it would make a better story, one he would eventually show at Kendal Mountain Film Festival. I felt more energised leaving for the next summit, but this stretch was still pissing me off. And I felt cross with myself for being a bit of an asshole. I was trying to make a joke of my misery to keep things light, but was still surprised these amazing friends of mine had not left me for dead, especially since I was now rather slow. I knew I needed to brighten myself up, but I was all out of ideas. On we slogged.

At the end of Watendlath's tedious bog was some bracken-bashing up to Great Crag. Surely that was all the bad bits done? It was an easier, grassy trot over to Grange Fell with a very small climb and I had the nice surprise of seeing Stephen Wilson with his camera on the summit. He takes beautiful photos so I tried to look my best. I like to compare the lovely, sunny shots Stephen takes with Steve's preference for capturing really gnarly weather. So of course Steve had been there when I was puffing on my Ventolin thinking I would gasp my last breath as the blizzard engulfed us on top of Robinson. Steve would literally climb any mountain for the perfect action shot.

I must have been distracted because it was my fault we took the wrong line off Grange Fell. I cursed myself as my tired feet struggled with steep ground and bracken I shouldn't have needed to cross. But there was no way

I was going back up, so I hobbled on down. *Positive thoughts. Come on, Sabs.* At least I didn't have to do three kilometres extra, as I had on the second attempt, as the River Derwent was relatively low and we could cross it there. Struggling up to Castle Crag, the last summit of the leg, I was pondering why I can never remember the way there, since it's really not that hard. As we pulled into Rosthwaite I had to fight to keep a lid on my mood when I realised the camper van was miles away, although in reality it might have been only 200 metres. My aching body didn't want to go a step further than it needed to.

That was the point where we began getting thin on supporters marked on the schedule. I had relied on the hope that if I got that far, people would be excited and would just come out to help. We always had my good friend Johnny Whilock as backup for any legs we were slim on. Johnny and I had spent much of the 2015 Dragon's Back running together. I really liked his company and his pace was about the same as mine. He was also excellent at navigating without being a male chauvinist. In fact, he possibly had too little self-belief, since at one point he followed me over a stile in completely the wrong direction. He'd even said it was the wrong way but I was absolutely adamant. So I trusted him now 100 per cent with the navigation on this tricky leg in the dark, a leg that was in fact my favourite as it included my favourite fell, Starling Dodd.

For this delight I had also invited my friend Robin Bush. He would meet us midway and be the packhorse, since he didn't want the responsibility of navigation for fear of getting it wrong (and facing the wrath of Sabs). Of course, I'd like to think I am a sweet, motivated, happy-go-lucky little soul, but others see this determined, feisty, intimidating woman. At that point, I was as focused as anything. I had fucked up the last leg, but not irretrievably. I was still on target but there was going to be no margin for error now. I had to press on.

ELEVEN

FOURTH TIME LUCKY

Johnny led the way as we climbed out of Rosthwaite up to Bessyboot in the dark. Hazel Clark stuck solidly by my side or dropped behind. She was ridiculously attentive despite my demands for food, water and chat. I was so glad Hazel was with me. She owns a massage company in Bowness but it would be an absolute injustice simply to call her a masseuse. She is a better physiotherapist than any I have used, with a multitude of skills, from myofascial release, acupuncture and massage to providing exercises for me to go home and work on myself. She's also a damned good listener and radiates positivity. I was pleased she was there because, despite having been full of self-doubt about her ability to keep up and be useful, she was proving that not only was she indispensable but she was in her element. I was so impressed with her strength to carry a weighty pack, and in turn she admired how I knew the mountains inside out. I could feel them in the dark and knew virtually every footstep I had to make to get me to the end.

Paul Nelson was there too, a bit like an excited spaniel running up to Johnny then back to us and all over the shop; he clearly had some excess energy to burn. Paul is ex-military, an extremely tough and capable guy. I ran with him on my first Lakeland 100 outing and since then we've raced each other in a few ultras and helped out on the same rounds and FKTs.

He'd come out to cheer me on in the Spine Race and had been a frequenter of my various Wainwright attempts.

I was going well, ticking off the summits: Glaramara, Allen Crags, Seathwaite Fell. Then a big drop and slog up Base Brown before the easy trot to Green Gable, followed by crappier ground up Great Gable. Maybe because I was feeling sleepy we took the wrong line off Great Gable, down technical, slippery stuff that was so bad Hazel sat down and didn't want to move. I couldn't blame her. I felt like doing the same. I wanted to throw a huge tantrum and chuck all my toys out of the pram.

Hold it together, Sabs, you are so close.

I told Hazel to take her time because the next bit was an out-and-back. She could catch us up on the return. I told myself this small error wasn't grave and to get a grip. At least the night was almost over, the fourth on this attempt, and my anger had woken me up. I tried to ignore the fact that I'd descended about fifty metres more than necessary and would now have to climb back up over some rough ground.

It was getting light on Kirk Fell, but it was a grey dawn, a bit damp and miserable, although once down and reunited with Hazel, my favourite fell was calling. Robin Bush was waiting for us on Grey Knotts as we whizzed round the familiar Bob Graham lines before diverting for Fleetwith Pike. Hazel and Paul left for Honister but Johnny soldiered on with the navigation while Robin was loaded up like a mule. I'd not run much with Robin but he was quick and kept drifting into my personal space. I chastised myself for my negative thoughts, reminding myself that he was here to help and doing the best he could. And he was doing an amazing job of providing everything I needed: food, water and chat. But while I was enjoying his company, I still felt a little nervous that he was about to crash into me. Then, as we descended from Hay Stacks, he did lose his footing and fell on me. I managed to catch myself before I came off the small ledge I was standing on.

'I've got you!' he shouted. I had to laugh.

Now all the technical sections of this leg were over, I was back on my favourite stretch of grassy goodness. I might not have had my sprinting legs on, but I could trot some of the flat and even slightly uphill parts. This was credit to Robin, who was force-feeding me at regular intervals. If you imagine eating 8,000 to 10,000 calories a day is fun, then try doing it for six days on the trot. My body was run down from the sheer stress of running and lack of sleep: prime conditions for mouth ulcers. And having consumed my own body weight in sugar without an overnight break, my mouth was rotten with them. At least I was brushing my teeth regularly, having put a folding toothbrush and small toothpaste tube in both fanny packs for my pacers to carry. But I was forced to eat boring food with a sore mouth.

The easiest things for me to get down were Mountain Fuel jellies, and miraculously they remained a favourite. But if these were all I consumed on this fourteen-hour leg, then I would need one every twenty minutes. That's a lot of jellies, and there were only so many of the things my poor pacers could carry. I was looking forward to getting to Loweswater for some proper food. However, having ticked off all my favourites, the beauties of Buttermere – High Crag, High Stile, Red Pike, Starling Dodd and Great Borne – I was now left with the ugliest: Hen Comb and Mellbreak. To be fair, approach these from the right direction and they are really quite runnable and lovely. But if you want to take the shortest, most efficient route, then you're in for a rough time. The only saving grace was that being early enough in June the bracken wasn't Sabs-high yet. Hen Comb wasn't too bad and we managed to take a nice line off it to the base of Mellbreak, but the slog across the bog was energy-sapping.

In the distance I could see two figures amongst the bracken, one with an unmistakable shepherd's crook in his hand. It was Joss Naylor. I couldn't believe this absolute legend of a man had come out to cheer me on. I have so much respect for him, not just for being 'King of the Fells' but because he is kind and supportive and has done so much good with his life. He still does: writing books, making films, racing and getting out to inspire people like me. How could I do anything but boss Mellbreak into submission? I felt Joss's expectant eyes on me, so I mustered my inner strength to clamber up the uneven ground, pushing through the vegetation and breaking a sweat, but we'd made it: the last summit on the leg.

Mike Robinson would be running the next leg with me for the third time. For attempts one and two, starting from Keswick, it had been third on the list. On the third attempt, because of starting in Langdale rather than

Keswick, it was leg twenty and I hadn't made it this far. Joining Mike was his wife, another Hazel, their three dogs and Steph Dwyer. I had met Steph on the Winter Spine Race in 2020, when she'd put me on a pedestal and that made it awkward to be friends. She had turned up to Moot Hall to see me in on my second attempt, but had thought I'd be cross because my tracking page had asked people to stay away due to Covid-19. We didn't want a crowd. I'm not sure how we eventually started hanging out, since I'm still stuck on this pedestal, but Steph and her fiancé Mike Bottomley were keen to help me on both the third and fourth attempts. They had also supported me on my Pennine Way FKT, lugging a lot of heavy kit and food up to a remote hut so I could have a fire and some hot noodles on a horrid day.

It was on this twentieth leg that I noticed I was having a problem with my waterworks. I needed to urinate, but when I tried nothing came out. I knew that wasn't good; it reminded me of the experience I had had on the Summer Spine. I decided I'd better drink more, and especially isotonic fluids, so we also added Mountain Fuel to my water. The conditions were hot, so I got as much down as I could, but I wasn't able to go as fast I wanted. I drank so much that I think everyone else thought I was being paranoid.

By the afternoon, when I reached Ennerdale, the day was a proper scorcher and I was really concerned about my condition. I knew I was close to my goal and didn't want to make any mistakes. I told Ben I was going to take half an hour in the camper van to sort myself out. I felt bad for keeping the pacers waiting, but it was a nice day and the midges weren't out, so I hoped they didn't mind. I ate some food and drank plenty of fluids and then got my head down for twenty minutes. When I woke up I managed to have a proper wee and it seemed a good colour: like chardonnay rather than straw but not clear. I felt ready to go on but still had concerns about how hot it was, so decided to make my ever-suffering pacers carry a shedload of fluids. At least I did drink them.

For the next leg I had Chris Lund supporting me, someone I'd met a few times on the Great Lakeland 3Day mountain marathon, as well as having him deliver biomass pellets to our bunkhouse in Great Langdale. Chris had once been happy participating in the B and C class of this race, but during lockdown had decided to get fitter and thinner. I'd not seen him for a while, so it was a bit of a shock to see how much weight he'd lost. He was excited for the challenge of taking on this long leg, taking about ten hours overnight. Kevin Barron was also on the support team, someone our mutual friend Darren Moore had persuaded to join me for the Kentmere to Martindale stretch on my third attempt. Kevin had been so brilliant I'd asked him to help me on this critical leg through the last night of my attempt. Dominic Farrell had also turned up unannounced, but I was delighted to see him. He quietly asked if it was okay to join the team for this leg. Yes, please! I didn't know him that well and now had the chance to find out a little bit more about this dark horse.

Of all the Wainwright attempts I made, this is the leg I look back on with the fondest memories. It was a beautiful evening. The climb up to Grike was hard in the heat, but once on top there was a breeze. I felt really good; my legs felt almost fresh. I was definitely giving my pacers a run for their money on the downhill. The ground was nice and dry, so it was easy to make progress. Dominic turned round before Caw Fell to get back to Ennerdale before dark.

We met Tim Ripper on the summit. Tim was scantily clad in shorts and a T-shirt, appropriate earlier in the day but not now the wind had picked up. I was wearing my PrimaLoft jacket. We were somewhat sheltered until Haycock but then had a full-on headwind that made progress harder. I started to feel weary around Steeple, so Tim decided to give me some fuel. He had brought a hot thermos of tea, a selection of fruit including strawberries, and some fresh cake from the local bakery. Wow! I couldn't believe I was having such a feast on top of this mountain and I was even more grateful as these delicious things were easy to get down. Re-energised, I was ready to tackle the wind again. Tim was a fount of local knowledge, finding easy trods and knowing which lines to take to shelter from the wind on our way to Pillar. The way back was easier with a crosswind instead of a headwind, but now it was dark.

We headed to Red Pike, taking the Bob Graham line to Yewbarrow and then dropping off the western slope to hit the gully precisely: my preferred line. Nailed it. The next bit was harder, especially in the dark. I had route options from here to Middle Fell but none of them were particularly appealing. They included the grimly steep bracken ascent from Steve's route, a new route I had found that was a bit longer but contoured round Knott End avoiding the crags, or apparently Tim's new 'fuck it, we'll just go in a straight line' option. It wasn't the fastest or easiest option, but it did get us there and I was too zonked to care. It was the first point on the round where I was really struggling to fight off the sleep demons. It was my fifth night and I had only had five hours' sleep. After staggering a little too much and failing to hold my eyelids up, I told Tim I had to stop and sleep for five minutes. According to the team, I sat straight down and went out like a light. When they woke me five minutes later, I was as bright as a button. The miracle of the micro-nap.

I was glad to reach the camper van at Nether Wasdale for a well-earnt sleep. I had hit this support point in the dark, having knocked at least an hour off my predicted split, making up time I'd lost on the earlier 'shit' Armboth leg from Keswick. This would be my last sleep on the round with only four legs to go: the toughest of all next and then three easy legs home. The start of the next day was a bit hazy but I do remember being really glad to meet the famously bare-footed Aleks Kashefi, although that morning he was wearing some kind of sandal contraption. I couldn't believe anyone would want to run in the fells, especially the technical, rocky trails on the Scafell range, without some solid protection over their toes – madness! Aside from that, given it was summer, it wasn't exactly warm. I had my full-length bamboo lite waterproof socks tucked inside my comparatively solid Mutants and my feet still felt the right temperature. They would not have enjoyed the fresh air. But if Aleks could manage this leg in sandals, then I had nothing to complain about.

Jim Bacon joined us too as we climbed out of Wasdale on that damp morning. I was relying on Jim to provide unending chatter that I wouldn't have to reply to but would keep me entertained on this arduous leg. I first met Jim through the Lonsdale Fell Runners and he accompanied me for the second leg of my Ramsay Round in June 2019. I had started suffering with asthma towards the end of the leg, coughing a lot and struggling to breathe, and like an idiot I had forgotten to bring my inhaler. I was going to sack it off at the end of the leg, but Jim wouldn't let me. I couldn't give up just because I had a little cough. His friend Rae-Ann was also waiting, keen to come with me over the Mamores. Given how early she'd got up, I figured I owed it to her. Pretty soon I was glad I'd listened to Jim. As I left the thick vegetation on the valley floor and headed up the hill away from the pollen, my breathing improved. It comforted me on this leg knowing I had Jim who wasn't going to take any shit from me about quitting – not that that was ever on the cards, but just in case the tough got going.

I was safely round 191 of 214 peaks with only about fifty kilometres left, but for the first time I experienced a niggle in my legs that wasn't just wear and tear. By the time we reached Slight Side it was mid-morning but it had actually got colder, not warmer, and was wetter and windier as well. I was getting a little chilly and stiffening up, but a pain in my right quad was new. It didn't hinder me too much at first, just annoyed me. I was hobbling a little coming off Scafell Pike, although glad that this time I'd taken my preferred route choice. The hike up Lingmell was fine, but as we descended the quad started aching more and I had to stop. I tried to stretch it out a bit and then Aleks suggested some crazy couch stretch, which we improvised by him becoming the couch. It didn't really help, so I decided to stop wasting time and get on with it. I was nearly there and it wasn't anywhere near as painful as the injury I had suffered on the second attempt.

I wasn't brave enough in those murky conditions to take the direct line I'd recced from Esk Pike to Rossett that contours round south of the tarn. Instead, I took the safer, longer route, which was probably better for my dodgy leg anyway. At that point I was really cold and wet and we'd run out of warm dry layers for me to put on. I could sense my home in Langdale only four kilometres away. As Steph Dwyer and Mike Bottomley had just joined us, I felt bad asking Mike to run down to my home and fetch me some clothes back up, but I knew he'd enjoy the challenge. He could descend Stake Pass to my house quickly enough and then climb back up to Red Tarn to catch us before we went up Blisco. The distance would be about ten kilometres, but while we would do about half that, it was gnarly over Crinkle Crags and I was moving quite slowly anyway. In the meantime, I ate lots of cake to keep the energy going in, not only to move forwards but also to help me generate heat. Mike made it in good time, catching us in the col, and Jim got his single-person tent out to shelter me from the rain while I changed.

It felt great being in dry clothes, but also disturbing to see how many wet layers I had taken off. I had been wearing everyone's spare layers, at least five jackets. No wonder I'd been going so slowly. All of them were sodden and collectively weighed a tonne. So it might have taken ten minutes or more to change but it was the right decision. Now I was warm, dry and light. My quad still hurt and now I had developed a little bulge in my thigh. Steph decided that rolling it out with a walking pole would help. I'm not sure what hurt more: Mike's ear as I screamed into it or my quad. So Steph came up with another idea. She filled one of my water flasks with hot water and I shoved it down my leggings against my quad. I didn't think it would work but I enjoyed the warmth of the hot-water bottle.

Unfortunately, my thigh was not only still hurting but slowing me down. Having winced along for a bit, I gave in and agreed to take a gram of paracetamol. I hadn't intended to use any painkillers, wanting to complete my round without drugs, but that was the exception. The painkiller definitely helped and I eventually got into the Hardknott Pass support point having taken around two hours longer than I should have. This was partly due to the terrible weather conditions, partly to the injury and partly to the faff of changing clothes and stretching.

I was glad to have made it: this was definitely the home run. I would definitely finish the round, and by then it was clear I would break Paul's record. But that wasn't enough. I was absolutely on the cusp of achieving my goal of breaking six days. But I was going to have to pull something quite special out of the bag to claim it. I had given myself a three-hour buffer in the schedule with some sleep time for the last overnight leg. I was going to have to forgo any sleep in order to finish on time. And if I stayed focused, I knew I could do it.

When I wrote the schedule I had no idea who would be able to come and run it with me. I would have chosen Tim Miller, who had recced it with me, or Shane Ohly, who had given me the party ring biscuits on my second attempt on this leg. I figured they were probably too fed up with me and my incessant obsession with the Wainwrights to come out yet again. Instead, I was so lucky to have Rachel Platt, Steph Dwyer and Chris

Swanepoel along. I frequently bumped into Rachel on the fells and we had mutual friends, but I didn't know her too well. Yet she still volunteered to come and support me on this leg and was happy to apply her magic massage hands at any support points she could get to. I remember drifting off to sleep in Ennerdale as Rachel massaged me, occasionally waking up with a grunt or shout as she pressed on something tender. I was impressed with her skills: she was gentle but firm enough for effect, patiently coaxing out the knots. My legs always felt better for her efforts. She made me realise how much benefit the massages offered. I regretted I hadn't been able to have this sort of treatment for most of the round, but then simultaneously felt like a diva when I did get it.

Chris was roped into this leg and the next one by his employers at Kong Adventure Centre in Keswick, my friends Lou and Paul. I had not met him before. He was clearly nervous, as Ben had put him in charge of navigation for the leg and I was the fire-breathing dragon lady who would scorch him alive if he got it wrong. I had tried to explain to everyone that the navigation was ultimately my responsibility and that if it went wrong it was my fault. I did appreciate them going ahead to scout the trail, but I really did know where I was going. In daylight on this leg it certainly wasn't going to be a problem. However, I was ferociously determined at that point. I was hurting all over and a bit grumpy and pushing myself slightly out of my comfort zone for the first time to get the challenge done.

It was time to put the hammer down and so I did. I would down a Mountain Fuel jelly then push myself into a jog; the going was easy so there was no excuse for walking. Occasionally it was a bit too much and I had to drop into a walk. Steph kept talking a lot and I was grumpy, even mean. I didn't know what I wanted: talk or silence. At one point the incessant chatter got to me so I asked her to go on ahead with Chris to find the route. We took a great line up Green Crag and then on the descent I felt bad about how I had treated her, so I asked Steph if she was okay.

'You're a bit quiet,' I said.

'That's because you told me not to talk.' I laughed. It's a miracle she's still my friend. I'm not sure why, but when I'm hurting I take it out on my nearest and dearest, like Steph and my husband. I apologise for my behaviour but they always brush it off, saying it's to be expected when you haven't slept for six days and are still pushing yourself to this level. But I still hate myself a little bit for it.

I ran strongly into Duddon End, knowing I had beasted the leg and was on track for my target of six days. I was welcomed by the jolly sound of Johnny Whilock's bagpipes: the sweet sound of a true friend. At Cat Bells, my final summit of the second attempt, I felt a brief pang of nostalgia, but at that moment I knew 100 per cent I'd bag all the Wainwrights in five days and something. *Don't fuck up now.* As we left the music behind, I realised we had picked up a couple of strays. They asked politely if they could come with us up Dow Crag. The more the merrier, I told them. Kat and Dougie are locals living in Coniston, inspired by my running and wanting to be part of the adventure. I admire their youth and enthusiasm. Kat had a music app open and asked me what song I'd like her to play. That's easy. *Eye of the Tiger*. If ever there was a tune to get me up the Dow Crag slog, that's the one. I'd got to stay awake! So there we were on a beautiful summer's evening rocking it all over the Coniston Fells and I was singing at the top of my lungs.

The song transported me back to a school hall at Tunbridge Wells in Kent when I took on my rival in epée in the varsity match for modern pentathlon. I remembered how it had filled me with adrenaline and I fought to the best of my ability to win.

We played more songs as Dougie and Kat came with us all the way to the Old Man before descending to Coniston. When they left, the sleep demons came, my lids grew heavy and I started to stagger. I knew I had to hold it together. Not far to go. I knew I had to push. I couldn't lose it but I was so tired. *Don't give in. Fight!* Josh Hartley had coffee, so I sipped some and slurped more Mountain Fuel jellies. I hated to think how many of them I had ingested on this round. (Someone had the idea – too late – of collecting all the wrappers to make a mound at the end. It would have been impressive.) Josh is a handy fell runner and knows the Coniston range like the back of his hand. I was so glad he could make it out again to support me: he'd been there with me on my second attempt over the Scafell range with Nicky Spinks. That had been a hard leg. It was miserably wet and pretty cold; the water in my flask was almost frozen. These benign conditions were easier but more inducive for falling asleep. There's nothing like a gusty wind to keep you awake.

On the plus side, my leg wasn't too bad. Rachel was with us for some of the section and gave me a quick massage on the hill before departing. I couldn't afford to stop and faff, so every stop had to be quick and productive: it had to achieve something. Otherwise, one foot in front of the other was the only thing to be done. I had to stay awake. In hindsight, I wonder how on earth I could even think of falling asleep so close to the end, but I had been going for five and a half days. I was pushing the limit of what was humanly possible in the sleep department because that was all I had. That was my secret weapon. *Please don't fail me now.*

Wetherlam summit. 211 of 214. Three peaks to go and I am absolutely bang on my schedule to arrive at 7.03 a.m. exactly six days after I started. As we descend off the fell, Tory slips and breaks one of my Leki poles, which she's been holding for me. She obviously feels terrible but I really don't care. I've got a spare pair at the next support point and don't need them here anyway. In fact it's faster without them.

Arriving at Tilberthwaite Quarry, the atmosphere seems a bit tense. I don't understand why. I know I'm going to do it. In the schedule I gave myself ten minutes here and I'm only going to use one minute, so I know I've got a nine-minute buffer. The reason for this nervous mood is only revealed to me later, when I read the WhatsApp message thread on my progress. Ben had updated the schedule and discovered I had lost time on the preceding legs. It was now projecting arrival time in Langdale at 7.08 a.m., five minutes over six days. There was a flurry of messages about how to keep me focused and on schedule to bring that down.

My team have burdened themselves with the responsibility of the success of the round, but it isn't their responsibility: it's mine. If I fail, it's my own doing. They have all played their parts and done all they can to get me to this point. But now only I can bully myself to the end.

The ascent up Holme Fell is tricky from this direction at the best of times, but in the dark and via my preferred shortcut it is impossible for

© Andy Jackson.

anyone who has not recced it. I feel bad for Paul Wilson, who is doing his utmost to lead the way, but I don't follow him. Instead, I follow my feet; they know where they are going. I had done this leg repeatedly because it is difficult and close to home and I knew it would almost certainly be in the dark, as it is now. Dawn arrives, promising another glorious day on the fell, but I won't be out here long. There are now just a couple of hours to go.

Hazel Clark meets us on the road crossing by Yew Tree Tarn. She feeds me a doughnut. It is the best doughnut I have ever tasted, apart maybe from the one I eat after that. The sugar rush goes straight to my legs and I increase the pace. Why haven't I thought of these as a good race snack before? Doughnuts are the perfect balance of sugars and more complex carbs, moist and easy to eat. They are almost as good as cake.

I've woken up in the morning sun and realise there are quite a few people with me now, so many good friends. On the last climb up to Lingmoor, I'm just enjoying the moment. I'm not in too much of a hurry now. I know I've got this, so I am savouring every minute of a glorious day. I am full of gratitude and joy for all the great friends I have and for all the generosity of the fell-running community. I tag my last summit, Brown How on Lingmoor Fell, which I can see out of the window at home, the one I know now will be special forever. And a huge grin spreads across my face as Andy Jackson captures the moment with his camera.

It doesn't matter that the descent is difficult and jolting my tired legs; I'm running home to a warm bath and rest. There's a very small gathering at 6.52 a.m. at the Sticklebarn, which is all I wanted. I'm glad to see Ben. I give him a big hug but I cannot celebrate. I thank my supporters. I smile. I'm happy. Then I toddle off humbly to my house. I'm not jubilant, just relieved I didn't let everyone down and their efforts weren't wasted. That I won't have to ask anyone to come out and help again. That I won't have to stare at the spreadsheet anymore. I don't feel glorious. I don't feel like I've won. I just feel satisfied. And content.

EPILOGUE

There was a lot of media attention after I broke the record. Once again the phone rang non-stop for interviews. I drove all the way to Salford to sit on the red couch with the *BBC Breakfast* crew. However, it wasn't until I received the Long Distance Award from the Fell Runners Association that I really considered my achievement. It was a huge honour to have the support of the fell-running community. I felt welcomed and embraced into this alliance. I'd always felt on the edge of things, not one thing or another, my mum being French and my dad Indian. I've never felt part of either culture. I run on the fells, but not quickly like true fell runners: more like an ultrarunner. Receiving the award felt like being voted into a club. I also felt I had put to bed anyone's concerns about the 'physical assistance' I had received on the previous round.

After the successful Wainwrights Round I did not allow myself much time to recover. I felt pretty good. My feet were perfect, my lungs were fine and my legs felt used, not abused. I felt an overwhelming need to give back and support my fellow runners with their own missions. I was inundated with requests to help on Bob Graham rounds, Wainwrights rounds and other FKT attempts. I always said yes unless one request clashed with another, even though I knew my body could barely take it.

Just two weeks after finishing the round, I headed up to the Highlands to support Kim Collison on his twenty-four-hour Munro record. Kim had asked me to support his final leg: 40.6 kilometres and 1,635 metres of ascent overnight, starting at midnight. I didn't imagine I'd be able to keep up with Kim at the best of times – and it certainly wasn't the best of times. However, I cunningly recruited a much more able-bodied and local fell runner, Al Hubbard, and my husband to help me. Ben and I travelled up in our camper van on the Thursday night and spent Friday with Al on a little recce. I was cautious not to overdo it and so was mainly walking to save my legs for the next day. Kim flew round the first three legs and was up almost an hour before heading out on the fourth to meet us at Glen Shee. However, as the clag came down and night set in, he thankfully slowed down, because if he had gained any more time we would have thought about adding another Munro to our leg, making it even longer.

It was an incredible night out. The clag was so thick we couldn't even see each other's head torches shining and it became too easy to lose one another in the thick mist. I committed myself to pushing on and being as useful as I could for the first part of the leg, forcing myself to keep up with Kim and make sure he was eating regularly. All he could really handle were Mountain Fuel jellies; he didn't want solids. After a couple of hours I knew I had to back my pace off, so I handed feeding duties over to Ben and cut out a couple of summits, taking a shorter line to rejoin the group.

It was a fabulous experience, breaking away from the group and being completely on my own in the night, in the dark, in the clag on hills I'd never visited before: a real adventure. I reached Tolmount and waited there while the others were on their way from Tom Buidhe. It was eerily quiet while I waited, in a gentle breeze and misty rain. At the previous summit, Kim had been thirty-five minutes up. I had reached this summit forty minutes up on his schedule. After standing there for twenty minutes, I started to wonder whether it was possible I had missed them. The cloud was so thick the summit cairn was barely visible. How long should I wait there, I wondered? If I waited too long and they were ahead of me, I'd never catch up again. I had signal and tried to ring Ben, but clearly he didn't. I reasoned they were not nearby and must be lower than me, therefore either still on their way or ahead and on the way to the next summit. I texted Ben I was leaving Tolmount so he would at least have an idea where I was. Then I panicked I was miles behind so cut across Fafernie, skipping more summits to be sure I really would get ahead of them.

Having reached Cairn Bannoch in good time, I realised I hadn't eaten or drunk anything all evening. But having munched on a bar and sipped some water, I started to get cold and so decided to head back along the route towards Broad Cairn, the direction the others would be coming. It seemed ages but eventually four runners appeared out of the clag and all was well. Kim was a little down on his splits so we had to put the hammer down. The rest of the team were exhausted, though, and only Al was able to continue with his much-needed navigational duty. Morning came, but that didn't help much as the mist was still thick. We ploughed on and while I was beasting myself up the next hill, I was also telling Kim to go faster. His response was amazing; he was already pushing but found that next gear and chugged on. As we pressed on up Lochnagar, the final Munro, I handed Kim his jelly sweets and told him I'd see him at the end. I was done.

Scrambling round the side of Lochnagar to try and catch them on the descent, I discovered the route was so rough with rocks and boulders that it was actually slower than if I'd stuck to the summit path. I knew I'd lost them. Finally, I reached a good track at the edge of Ballochbuie Forest and, gathering every last ounce of energy, I tried to sprint down and catch them. I wanted to get myself in before the twenty-four-hour deadline of 6 a.m.; not that it actually mattered for Kim's record, but it was my way of willing him on in spirit. Just before reaching the finish point, Invercauld Bridge, I received a text message from Ben to say that they were in a car park half a mile up the road. 'He made it!' Fantastic: I could stop running.

I felt like I'd used more effort in that feat than in anything I'd ever tried to achieve for myself. I was goosed. Over the next few weeks I realised that my running in Scotland had definitely been too much too soon, but I had no time to rest. The next outing was to support John Kelly on his first bid to break my Wainwrights record. I wanted to help in any way I could. John hadn't been able to assist on my fourth attempt, but he'd been a huge part of the third attempt and, like Kim, is a fellow La Sportiva teammate.

I walked over to Wasdale from Langdale the day before the leg and stayed at the Church Stile campsite with Aleks, who had supported me on my fourth round. Then, next morning, I walked to Nether Wasdale to do the Scafell leg to Hardknott with John.

It was a baking hot day, just as I like it. I joined the rest of the support team at the bottom of Buckbarrow, basking in the sunshine, waiting for John. He wasn't enjoying the heat, but we'd got some ice and cold packs for him and even some ice cream. John arrived a couple of hours behind schedule but wanted to sleep for a bit, so we waited some more. I sat there nervously hoping that my legs would work. John had asked me to do this particular leg with him because he knew it was difficult to navigate. Like me, he was reluctant to descend West Wall Traverse, the route Steve Birkinshaw and Paul Tierney had taken between Scafell and Lingmell. I preferred a route I'd found one day that picks up a climber's traversing line around the east side of Scafell Buttress. As I knew the route, I offered to navigate, since I was going to be no use as a mule. I knew it was going to be another tough outing and I didn't want to let him down.

John battled on in the heat but it took its toll. His feet had blistered up so much by the time he got to Ullscarf that he decided to call it a day. He'd run hard for two days and made it to 85 out of 214 peaks. He'd taken fifty hours and one minute to get to Ullscarf from Moot Hall; Paul Tierney had taken fifty-three hours and twenty-four minutes back in 2019. However, Paul had already bagged about eight hours' rest by this point, whereas John had had barely an hour. After this attempt, it felt uncertain to me whether John could actually break my record. There was a sigh of relief from a few of my supporters. Perhaps they felt that after my four attempts, my record deserved to hold on a little longer. However, I had got caught up in the enthusiasm and buzz of supporting John and felt the usual downer of being part of a failed attempt.

The fell-running community is a unique one. Perhaps it is the appreciation of the potential hazards of the mountains and weather that brings us together. I don't know one fell runner who wouldn't sack off a race to help a person who needed assistance in the hills. It's satisfying and enjoyable to come together as a team and support one person's bid for a record, even if it's your own. I was happy to help John for a second time on his bid for the Wainwrights record. I wanted to see first-hand what he could do. I could see he was confident that not only would he beat my time but he would be aiming for that five-day barrier. I knew that was ambitious, but I admired his courage for pushing the bar higher.

In May 2022 I was back on Cat Bells. This time it wasn't for my last summit but John's. It was an incredible evening; there wasn't a breath of wind and the sun was setting. John turned to me and said cannily, 'I'm feeling sleepy, do you think I should have a nap?'

'Good idea! Perhaps we should set up a tent with a nice warm sleeping bag and you can have a good night's rest and maybe we'll get you up in twelve hours' time?'

I was teasing him and also trying to assess how with it he was. He looked at me with a little grin.

I said, 'Come on, John, let's get this done. We're going to Moot Hall and you're going to have smashed my record by almost twelve hours!'

The atmosphere was buzzing as we pulled into the market square in Keswick. I joined Steve Birkinshaw as we disappeared anonymously into the crowd, looking up at the new 'Wainwrights hero' downing his pint on the Moot Hall steps. It had been an unexpected but incredible feat, bringing the record down to five days, twelve hours, fourteen minutes and forty-two seconds. I was happy for John: my teammate, my friend, my fellow fell runner. And anyway, I was still Queen of the Wainwrights.

I'm washing dishes, pots and pans in the kitchen and I realise I am now enjoying this mundane task, one I used to loathe, along with all house-keeping duties that are endless. It seems the voracious appetite I had for running in the mountains has been satisfied and I no longer hunger to be in the hills all the time. Instead I am turning my hand to neglected duties that I've pushed aside to make way for my running. I'm looking back at the last few years – all that I've done and all that I've achieved – and I feel a complete peacefulness within me.

The last few weeks of being asked by almost everyone I met 'What's next?' have made me realise that they might have an insatiable appetite, but do I? My answers have been varied and vague, from 'I have an entry to the Winter Spine Race' to 'I'm going into hibernation'. In truth, I don't know right now what I will do. I have an interest in mapping out a route for the Birketts in the same way that Steve Birkinshaw mapped the Wainwrights route. I suspect the 541 summits might take about two weeks to visit as a continuous round. The Munros are also calling: so many hills to run, so many adventures to live. I am grateful that running has given me so much: friends, fitness, focus and fun. The hills continue to inspire me and I can't wait for my next challenge. For now, my obsession with the Wainwrights has been put to bed, but I wouldn't say I've done my last round.

About three weeks after the first time I finished the Wainwrights, on my second attempt, there was a story in the newspaper about a St Bernard dog that had been helped off Scafell Pike by mountain rescue. My mum was fascinated with this story and called me.

'Did you see they rescued a dog off a mountain?'

'Yes I did see that; our mountain rescue team are truly impressive and I'm glad they got the dog down safely.'

'Have you ever been up that mountain?'

'Scafell Pike? Yes, in fact I did that one three weeks ago, along with 213 other peaks in the Lake District. That was also in the paper, by the way.'

'Are you sure you went up that one?'

'Yes I definitely did that one.'

'But it's really big.'

'Yes it's the biggest one and it's actually quite close to my house. I've been up it quite a few times.'

'What, all the way to the top?'

I thought of my mum, with her blue eyes and blonde hair, at the place I still automatically call home. How, when I ring her up because I am worried or upset, she won't be sympathetic but instead will break the problem apart into little chunks and suggest ways in which I can fix it. And that's exactly what I do.

Then I said, 'Do you know what? You're right, Mum, that one was just too big, so I did all the others and left that one out.'

ACKNOWLEDGEMENTS

Thank you to Steve Ashworth who, together with Matt and Ellie Green from Summit Fever Media and the support from La Sportiva, Berghaus and Right Lines Communications, created some fantastic footage of the third and fourth attempts. The daily film updates and the *All For One* film that Steve made allow me to share my experience of the fells with friends and family who have never ventured into the hills. The film is available on Vimeo.

Thanks also to:

La Sportiva for providing incredible shoes – Mutants – which meant I was able to run for six days without a single painful blister.

DexShells for an assortment of waterproof socks that kept my feet clean and dry in the muddiest and wettest conditions.

Berghaus for providing the ultimately lightweight and breathable waterproofs to keep me dry in all weathers.

Right Lines Communications for all the PR work and keeping everyone up to speed on my rounds.

Mountain Fuel for the mountains of jellies I consumed on my round, not to mention all the recovery shakes afterwards.

Supernatural Fuel for some easily digestible nutrition.

Petzl for the irreplaceably good NAO headlamp.

Leki poles

Lyon Equipment for all the support and the great job you do of supporting the niche brands.

Mountain Massage for keeping my legs in tip-top shape as well as helping me recover.

Open Tracking for the trackers so that people could watch my little dot on the move and my team knew where I was so they could meet me in the right place at the right time.

Ginger Bakers for all your fab tray bakes and cakes that fuelled me on my rounds.

A huge thank you to all the many people that contributed in some way to helping me on my rounds. I am so grateful to my support team on the fell and at road support points mentioned below but also to all the people that have encouraged me by cheering me on, watching my dot and for all the lovely messages on social media. Thank you all – it meant a lot!

So a special thank you to Ben Abdelnoor, Steve Ashworth, Penny Attwood, Jim Bacon, Lucie Barnes, Kevin Barron, Chris Baynham-Hughes, Matt Beresford, Steve Birkinshaw, Alastair Black, Rob Bond, Mike Bottomley, Robin Bush, Hazel Clark, Jim Clark, Mark Clarkson, Kim Collison, Paul Cornforth, Dave Cumins, Helen Davis, Maggie May Dempsie, Wendy Dodds, Howard Dracup, Dan Duxbury, Steph Dwyer, Andy F., Joe Falkner, Dominic Farrell, Sally Fawcett, Christine Findlay, Adam Firth, Astrid Gibbs, Tom Gibbs, Ian Grace, Caroline Graham, Colin Green, Ellie Green, Matt Green, Tom Hare, James Harris, Josh Hartley, Charlotte Hattersley, Charmian Heaton, Joe Hobbs, Tom Hollins, Martin Holroyd, Andy Jackson, Aleks Kashefi, Kat and Dougie from Coniston, John Kelly, John Knapp, Valerie Knapp, Chris Lines, Chris Lund, Adam Marcinowicz, Fiona Marley Paterson, Tim Miller, Tory Miller, Simon Mills, Darren Moore, Claire Nance, Joss Naylor, Paul Nelson, Scott Newburn, Lucy Noble, Shane Ohly, Ian Oldham, Lou Osborn, Tom Philips, Alex Pilkington, Rachel Platt, Jeff Powell Davies, Gaynor Prior, Jess Richardson, Beth Ripper, Charlotte Ripper, Tim Ripper, Hazel Robinson, Mike

Robinson, Giles Ruck, Jackie Scarf, Phil Scarf, Mingma Tsering Sherpa, Andy Slattery, Claire Smits, Jacob Snochowski, Sabina Snochowski, Peter Sowerby, David Spence, Nicky Spinks, Charlie Sproson, Nic Sproson, Elizabeth Stephenson, Laura Stephenson, Mel Steventon, Martin Stone, Chris Swanepoel, Neil Talbott, Natalie Taylor, James Thurlow, Paul Tierney, Peter Todhunter, Jacob Tonkin, Rachel Towe, Ben Turner, Craig Tweedie, Jonathan Whilock, Debs White, Rick White, Scott White, Stephen Wilson, Paul Wilson, Philip Withnall and Madeleine Wood.

I have a lot to thank Vertebrate Publishing for and those who worked with us to produce the book. Kirsty Reade contacted me to ask if I would be interested in writing a book about my various attempts at running the Wainwrights. I have always wanted to write a book but without this nudge I don't think I would have got around to it. It has been a very rewarding experience working with this unique set of individuals that have worked tirelessly to help me produce a book that we can all be proud of. So I would like to thank them all for their contributions:

Emma Lockley – editing
Jane Beagley – graphic/cover design
Rosie Edwards – artwork/layout
Shona Henderson – ebook and audiobook
Lorna Brogan – marketing
Moira Hunter – proofreading
Simon Norris – maps
Ed Douglas – editing

Just to acknowledge as well a few special gifts I've been given for running the Wainwrights:

Pip Conlon (Menaiart) – thank you for the beautiful felt fell of Starling Dodd you made me.

Peter Knowles (Rivers Publishing) – thank you for the jigsaw puzzle of the Wainwrights which I very much enjoyed putting together.

Robin Rutherford – thank you for the stunning wooden shield trophy you made me to commemorate my round.

Maddy Wood – thank you for your amazing and massive three-tiered cake which I enjoyed eating, shame there's none left, eh?!

Harveys Maps – thank you for providing me with a huge map of the Wainwrights, something I will treasure forever.

ABOUT THE AUTHOR

Sabrina Verjee lives in the heart of the Lake District, where she spends a lot of time running in the fells she loves. She has a background in adventure racing and modern pentathlon but is best known as an ultrarunner. She set a female record for the Pennine Way in 2020, was the overall winner of the 2019 Summer Spine Race, and has finished the ultra-endurance Dragon's Back Race three times. Fuelled by a love of cake and supported by her husband Ben and a team of fell-running friends, Sabrina made four attempts on the 214-peak Wainwrights Round, and in June 2021 became the first person to complete it in under six days. She runs her own independent, small-animal veterinary practice in Lancashire, which provides twenty-four-hour care to emergency patients. *Where There's a Hill* is her first book.